LIVE CYCLE

Straight from a desk, an attempt to cycle France with no training, no maps and no accommodation. For a friend, a charity - the full story

By

Andrew Wallace

Copyright © 2017

INTRODUCTION

I stood up from my desk, adjusted my shirt for the belly that hung over my belt and drove the quarter of a mile home to eat my pizza tea. My brand-new bike was waiting and I had decided, next week, I was going to cycle 1000km from the north of France to the south. No accommodation was booked, no route was planned and no training had been done. What could go wrong?

The trip turned into a daily adventure with laughs and challenges that each day led to the loss of something. My daily blog for family and close friends drew an audience larger and larger and people were gripped by the daily adventure, laughing out loud. Friends abroad were driving miles to find Wi-Fi so they could find out what happened next. Write a book they said. So here it is – the expanded material and the things I didn't want to say in a blog my mum was reading.

The most important reason for the trip was to support my friend who had been left suddenly sightless, learning to live in a world of darkness after a lifetime of light. He was ill and we planned to do the trip together but events overtook us. This book is for him.

TABLE OF CONTENTS

Legal Notes

All the people in this book are real and all events genuine. Where possible they have been consulted on their inclusion.

Chapter 1. A cross between Mr. Bean and Basil Fawlty

I'm not an athlete and I am not fit. I'm a 54, fat bellied, desk sitting, lift taking, car driving, TV watching, beer drinking, knee hurting man. I have not worn well and my son's friends think I am his grandfather. My clothes hang in the wardrobe in the hope that one day I will fit them again. In the last year I lost weight in an unconventional method – I turned muscle to flab which I can recommend as the worst diet plan ever. By doing less exercise I found I could lose weight but I'm now at the point where that doesn't work anymore.

I like to cycle - but just to the pub and in shorts and a T-shirt. This is my exercise regime. The new pub app on my phone gets the food and drink delivered to the table so I am never without drink. Sadly, I now describe the days to my family by the specials on the menu - fish Friday, chicken Wednesday or curry Thursday. There was a gap in my life as Monday's were unnamed but they are now Mexican Monday.

At this point it is probably useful if I give you some background as to my cycling and nature as that will then explain the subsequent chapters. I feel pleased about this as this is called foreshadowing and Shakespeare used it so I'm feeling pretty professional. My mum thinks I am Basil Fawlty, which kind of sums up how I looked in my younger days, and my wife thinks I am Mr. Bean, which kind of describes my dress sense. In my work, I am the only person who wears a shirt and tie and, like Mr. Bean, I have worn the same style for many years. I actually still have my very first teddy so that description is more accurate than I thought. Teddy was my first friend and friends are important.

So, some more foreshadowing with some stories from my life. A group of us cycle on a Sunday. The rules are quite simple - no lycra, no one to go over an average 8mph and "20's plenty" in terms of mileage. We can sometimes look like travelling tinkers or extra's from "Last of the Summer Wine". My friend Gordon started us pub cycling and over the years the routes have shortened and the pub arrivals got earlier. We discovered that pubs licensed as hotels open earlier than 12:30 on a Sunday and sometimes a little knowledge can be a dangerous thing. However, some cycling is better than no cycling and we would do 20 miles cycling to local towns, enjoying a few pints, watch the lunchtime football and then get a train home.

On one of Gordon's cycle's, over a few drinks in the pub, I suggested cycling abroad for a long weekend and, as one of life's organisers, I found myself planning a cycle trip in the Spanish Pyrenees. This always impressed other cyclists when I told them we were cycling the Pyrenees. But even in these days I wasn't an athlete as we paid the tour company to take us high into the mountains from where we would then cycle down to Girona and the Mediterranean Sea at Costa Brava. The route would follow the old railway line that had been converted to a cycle way so was traffic free and downhill. It still qualifies as "cycling the Pyrenees" though. There was one run where I freewheeled the entire day which actually wasn't as much fun as it sounds.

We started that trip in the cool mountains in a town called Ripoll, recently famous for its ISIS inspired terrorists and then cycled downhill to Olot, famous for its potatoes and four volcanoes. I dragged my friends around the volcano museum (much to their boredom) while killing time before going to the pub. Weird and wonderful things always happen on my trips and this very first trip was a prelude to what was to come.

We went into this bar, so narrow that there is only room for the bar down one wall and tables down the other. The tapas is cheap and delicious. It's not a tourist town so its "local prices" for beer and food. We ask if we can play cards and the owner starts shouting and gesturing. The other locals in the bar shout and gesture in agreement with him but I've no idea what he is saying. Perhaps cards are not allowed. I try to explain that it is not for money but he grabs my arm and leads me to the back of the pub. I don't need the toilet and I'm not sure where he is taking me. My two friends follow. He pulls aside a heavy red curtain and takes me through a door. I am now standing in a Spanish Tardis and look across a sea of card tables with pensioners playing cards. The owner shouts out and a group of pensioners clear a table and he beckons us to sit down. We had been in a narrow pokey pub and suddenly we are in this huge annex with maybe 100 people. The card table has the green Subbuteo type cover and is perfect for our game of Clag.

Clag is a card game I was brought up on and was first played at the Battle of Britain in 1940. Pilots would play the game which is a cross between whist and trump. Clouds Low Aircraft Grounded (CLAG). My grandparents, parents and cousins all played this game which crossed generations in the same way as the Wii does now. My friends loved it. So we had a great night playing cards surrounded by crowds of Spanish pensioners eager to see this game from the Battle of Britain.

The next day we cycled – downhill – into Girona. As luck would have it was the last Saturday in October, when the Spanish have their Halloween celebrations with fireworks. In these days there was no Internet and every time we arrived somewhere I would head for the tourist office to see what there was to see. I was told that there was a Halloween celebration in town with fireworks at 6pm, after dark, and we agreed we wanted to go. We turn up in the old town square ready for the fireworks. It seemed a bit strange as we stood there waiting in the crowd as everyone else was dressed up in layers of clothes with long sleeves and jackets. The Spanish are used to heat and were always wrapped up more than us but this seemed excessive. People in this town also seemed poor as the clothes looked old. We found it warm and so stood out as tourists in short sleeves and light clothes. Everyone was gathered in front of the church recently used in Game of Thrones as Kings Landing. (If you have ever watched Game of Thrones you will know what kind of streets are in Girona old town - narrow and cobbled.) A drum starts to beat and you can feel the emotion of the crowd rise. Suddenly the street lights go off. All the lights. We are in the old town and there are no lights. More drums beat, the noise echoing off the buildings. People all around us start putting on hats and pulling masks over their mouths and noses. A bang. A scream. Flares fire out from somewhere and the drummers turn into the main square from the corner of the church followed by goblin type creatures. The crowd starts to retreat and we stand bemused trying to understand what is happening. A huge bang this time and fireworks fire into the crowd and explode. What the? On the stairs of the cathedral I make out some figures and they are firing into the crowd with a kind of bazooka held at waist height. The lead drummer steps aside and the man behind has a 6-foot pole with ribbons from the top like a maypole. But the ribbons are ropes and the ropes are on fire. He swirls the pole and globules of oily fire spurt into the crowd and over us. OWW! It's like a bee sting on my arm. The crowd now runs down the narrow street they are being herded into. The goblin creatures run at us and we have to run too. They chase us. It's mayhem as the old town is a maze of alleys and narrow cobbled streets all in darkness. All the shops are boarded up. Why didn't I see that before? The creatures have a flame thrower device spurting out fiery sparks and the pole man keeps swinging the flaming nodules of oil. Creatures throw bangers and firecrackers at us and the air is thick with smoke. OW. OW. The oil hits my skin. My friend has his jacket over his head and round his face and I put on mine as my arms are stung. It's no good as the oil burns through the light material. Later it looks like bullet holes when I hold my jacket to the light. The noise, the smoke, the danger, the blackness. Have they never heard of health and safety? We are chased up and down streets and alleys for half an hour and any attempt at hiding in doorways is foiled by firecrackers and goblins throwing bangers at you. Eventually we get to the Ramblas and cross the bridge to safety. At the end there is a celebration in a square where large structures spurt out fire which we watch from a café.

I later discover that we had been in a "Correfoc" which is a Spanish bull run but with fireworks – look this up on Youtube for Girona to see what we went through. We didn't realise it, as we ran through the streets of Girona, but this was just the first of many amazing experiences and things that would happen that we would remember for the rest of our lives.

So, we would go every weekend cycling together and have cycle trips abroad two or three times a year. Four of us including Gordon were the core and over the years others joined us on trips. After doing this for a number of years we decided to cycle Cuba to celebrate 3 significant birthdays in the group.

Cuba is a communist country and everything is controlled with no possibility of independent travel so we had to book with a bike tour company. It is an amazing country with wonderful people. But it's hot. Very hot and we didn't cope well in the heat. On the first day of cycling I had my valuables in a bag on the back of my bike. The guy leading the tour would stop every so often for photos and water intake then hurry us up to move on. It was so hot that I put my day money and cards in the bag with the backup money and cards. The Cuban roads are a bit potholed and it was bumpy but refreshing coming down the hill but not so good climbing the next hill in the heat. At the top of the hill I looked for my bag and it was gone. Passport, wallet, glasses, hearing aid batteries, visa and everything of importance. The guide cycles down the hill and there is no sign of my valuables. Someone reports a car stopping, picking the bag up and driving off. This is day one and I am in rural Cuba, a communist country that has no shops, no opticians, no banks and, I discover later, no British staff in the British embassy. Without my visa I cannot leave the country. I have a hidden emergency third bundle of cash in my suitcase. But I have to wear sunglasses the rest of the trip which you would think is lucky in the Caribbean but at night there are no street lights in Cuba and I stumble around wearing my sunglasses in the dark. The batteries in my hearing aids give up two days later and I am unable to hear properly.

Cuban society is a cultural experience where they tell you everything is fine when it's actually not. I am reassured by the tour guide - the embassy have been informed, a new passport will be waiting for me in Havana and everything is organized. Over the next few days I lose confidence in this reassurance. The police will not file a report on the lost property and threaten to arrest the Cuban guide we have. I phone the British Embassy. The embassy, who I am assured by my Cuban guide know everything about my situation, have never been informed and there is no passport waiting for me in Havana. Furthermore, they state they will be closed for the weekend and they only open in the morning on Saturday. My flight is the day after. I leave the tour trip immediately accompanied by a friend who is concerned for my safety – I have good friends – and get a bus to Havana. At the bus stop we have an hour to wait and I chat in my limited Spanish to the locals. I play Scottish music though my Bluetooth speaker and we end up having an impromptu ceilidh with some Cubanitas.

In Havana the staff are Cuban and do not accept Sterling. This is the British Embassy I protest but they say I have to change the money. I can't change money without a passport. I can't get a passport without changing money. We go to a local bank and my friend changes the money. I get back to the embassy. "Where are your photos?" they say. No-one told me that I needed photos. I expected them to look up the computer and pull up my photo. There are no shops in Cuba but this is the embassy district so things are a little different. I get the passport photos from a shop nearby. A shop in Cuba! I get back to the embassy and the guy shakes his head "Fill out this form" he says. I get out my phone to find the details needed and the guard says "no phones". I move to go outside to fill in the form and he says "the form cannot be taken out". Cuba. Eventually I manage to get all this done and pass the form over. "Come back on Wednesday" he says. Today is Saturday and the flight is tomorrow. I explain the situation and he shakes his head. "I will see what I can do" he says. Five minutes before the embassy is due to close and he is still not back. I consider my options and decide I will refuse to move until I get my passport. Plan B is another week in Cuba which after all is an island paradise. Four minutes later I get my passport. I'm going home. And that, dear reader, is the second foreshadow.

I have good friends who are very supportive and, for me, are role models. My friend who left the tour missed out on the end of his holiday – I said I would be fine in Havana – but he insisted. Just as well as I would have missed my plane without him. Which brings me to my friend Gordon who on my many holidays with my wife always insisted on taking us to the airport and meeting us on return. Being seen off and getting welcomed home always topped and tailed a holiday nicely. Gordon is one of these really genuine people who would do anything for his friends. And he was a great laugh.

I worked in the same office as Gordon and when my son did his work experience from school Gordon challenged him to the Kick the Fridge Competition. You stand at one end of a long office, kick a football and have to hit the fridge at the other end.

Every new person does it. So, my son is invited to do the same by Gordon. My son is tall and powerful and plays football. It's a long kick from one end of an open plan room between the desks to the postage stamp sized fridge at the other end. He takes off his shoe. Gordon is worried and stands by the windows, just in case. My son looks at the fridge, looks at the ball and looks at the fridge. He runs and kicks the ball past Gordon's head, past the last desk heading for the fridge. It swerves slightly in the air as it drops from head height and the ball bounces off the fridge door. The first person ever to do that. I am now known as the Fridge Kicker's Dad. And Gordon gave him that memory. I have good friends.

Chapter 2. The bucket list trip

Gordon got a fright last year with the discovery of a benign tumour that could have been there for 20 years. Both of us had fancied cycling France after we retired. This was a wake-up call to do it now. We negotiated three weeks off our work and checked out the prices. No route would be planned no accommodation booked. We would set off and decide each day where we wanted to go in a general direction south. But Gordon's tumour got worse, affecting his vision. Very quickly. An operation was scheduled and the tumor removed. When Gordon opened his eyes, it was night and the lights were off. Except they weren't. The operation had left him blind. Can you imagine that? A lifetime of sight and you wake up blind. I can't. That was a big shock to everyone and difficult days. We wanted to do and say the right thing, to give some kind of comfort. We worried over saying the right thing – don't say "see you later" we practiced in our heads. Nothing. You can do nothing without sight. No smartphone, no TV, no radio without being able to see the LCD display, no newspaper, no book. Darkness. No idea of the ward you are in, the shape, the objects. I remember the fairground haunted house from my youth with the shaky floors and objects brushing my face and I try to imagine Gordon's world.

I tour the shops to find a radio for Gordon but they all have LCD displays that cannot be used by a blind person. I look up the Royal National Institute for the Blind website and radios are £240. That's seems a lot. I email a friend who does Talking Newspapers for the Blind and they source someone willing to lend me their radio with a dial and buttons. The kindness of strangers always amazes me. So now Gordon has Radio Scotland and the radio with its dials sits beside his bed. I cycle in to visit every morning sometimes getting things for him, sometimes finding him asleep and sometimes leaving a banana for him to enjoy later. It's a high dependency ward and the nurses are good about letting me in.

Before the operation there was some hope that Gordon and I would do the trip. A post operation train journey, three weeks fresh air, exercise and good food could be just the tonic. But blind? It wasn't happening. Gordon suggested I still go. I wanted to do the trip but no-one else in the cycling circle had the holidays, or freedom, to take three weeks out. In my younger days, I travelled alone overland from Scotland across Europe, through the Soviet Union to China and solo wasn't a problem for me. I decided would go by myself and stay in hostels or campsites where you always meet people from other walks of life, or at cheap chain hotels when I wanted to recharge. It would be more expensive than going with Gordon as costs would not be shared but life was telling me not to put things off. I spoke to Gordon as I felt guilty – I wouldn't be around and I was going on the trip he could not. Like he did not have enough to deal with he says "I want you to go and tell me all about every day when you get back"

I had already been saving for the trip, filling an old sweetie jar with lose change every night. I take it to the bank and am amazed to find I have £452. That will pay for my accommodation: no tent for me! I had the time booked off at work and there were two weeks before my departure.

A colleague at work says I should do this for charity and that people would be really keen to contribute. I'm reluctant as I hate asking people for money. But the Royal National Institute for the Blind (RNIB) have been really helpful and the sponsorship is a way of showing support for Gordon. JustGiving.com have a website that all charities use for this kind of thing so I set myself up on that. My colleague who encouraged me is the first person to sponsor me towards the £150 I set as the target. The last time I asked for sponsorship I was doing the Edinburgh Evening News charity walk in 1976 at £1 each. I decided that 40 years later £150 seems ambitious yet achievable. I get my first email from JustGiving and there is an error. Instead of £2 sponsorship it says £20. I check the web page and that says £20. What's going on? But she has contributed £20 and it's a great start. I'm at £115 at the end of the first day.

My mum says she will miss me as I speak to her every day. She doesn't want me to go and says it is too dangerous on my own. Gordon wants to hear about progress too as do my friends and colleagues. I am encouraged to do a blog and so set about creating that. I set it up and test I can do the daily updates from my phone It's a busy week before I leave.

I need to take clothes for three weeks and be able to carry it all. Packing does not take long as from my younger days I know the drill when carrying your own stuff. Put out what you need and then throw away half. I have two pannier bags and pack one only. If it doesn't fit the one bag it doesn't go. Wash and wear is my thought. Also, I'm travelling alone, if you get my drift

So, I have a general plan to head south, no accommodation booked, just a train and a ferry to Ouistretham on the Normandy beaches. I have not done any training as I only just decided to go. I think that if it gets too much I'll take a train or just give up and sit on the beach. I decide that my training will be the daily cycle. A few years back I could manage 30 miles in a day and that is the distance between towns. Perfect.

On the Wednesday before I leave, I look up accommodation for Friday and find every bed in every hotel within 50 miles of Ouistretham is booked. What's going on? I am due to arrive at 9:30 pm and I need somewhere to stay. I checked accommodation at the beginning of the week and there were plenty rooms. It turns out I have selected the Friday of the English half term holiday. A heat wave has arrived since I looked on Monday and everyone and their dog is off to France. A dog kennel might be where I am sleeping. A friend of mine sleeps in bus shelters when cycling but I don't fancy that. I have heard of a website for cyclists where people put you up for free. I download and use the warmshowers.org app and contact a woman with family who has accommodation near the ferry terminal. She doesn't reply so I contact a separate person not far from the ferry. Hopefully they'll get back in touch. Perhaps I can sleep on the beach?

On Thursday, I put an email round colleagues at work about the trip and the fundraising page and by night time the total sponsorship is at £575. That evening, I meet with Gordon and friends in the local pub for a bon voyage meal. A good few laughs. I still do not know where I am sleeping the next night but I am going.

During the evening I hear about the great work RNIB have been doing to help my friend adapt. Pretty glad I'm doing this.

An early start and I cycle into town at 04:30 passing the local pub. At the Roseburn Bridge I get a fright from 30 flocking pigeons that had been sleeping on the pavement. At Waverley Station, the 15-carriage train I'm booked on has all the cheap tickets in one carriage, with people crammed in like sardines, so I pick myself a table for four in one of the other 14 of the mostly empty, unreserved train. My bike is booked for free in the guard's van and it's all starting off well.

The restaurant car opens and they sell bacon rolls so I decide to treat myself. I'm on holiday and two people gave me envelopes of money for the trip. The restaurant car has just opened and they can't find the password for the till. "Take it for free" he says. Another good omen. A free breakfast!

The accommodation tonight is now sorted with a French family in Luc-sur-Mer right on the Normandy beaches and I'm staying for free. Nobody believes this when I tell them but cyclists are a hospitable lot. I actually got two offers of accommodation but choose the family over the single young female! I can't go empty handed and they ask me to bring shortbread as payment.

I'm amazed at the generosity of people on the Just Giving charity site as the fund continues to build and messages are left for Gordon. RNIB are also impressed and have emailed me asking if I can pop into their HQ in London when I get to Kings Cross. As it is on the way to Waterloo for the ferry train, I agree. They want some publicity photographs and to give me some stuff.

London is amazing with the number of bikes and Boris Johnstone has done a fantastic job creating safe cycle lanes through the centre of London. Electric hybrid, red, double deck buses quietly move around the streets with their mixture of electricity and diesel fuel. It's 10 minutes to the RNIB HQ and I'm waiting in their reception.

The RNIB was founded in 1871 by Dr Armitage and I learn there is a connection to France as he was raised at Avranches in Normandy France, attended the Sorbonne in Paris and King's College London. He became a physician, practicing at the Marylebone Dispensary, during the Crimean War, and as a private consultant in London. He was forced to abandon his medical career because of deteriorating vision, eventually becoming blind. He campaigned to adopt the French system of Braille to standardize the way of reading books in Britain. The RNIB became the leading charity for improving the life of blind people in Britain and Queen Victoria was their first patron.

Bindy and Hannah are the two RNIB fund raisers who contacted me and they arrive in reception with a bundle of clothes and items to give me. I'm carrying all my luggage with me so I politely decline everything except the shirt which I will wear at key points for photos. They are amazed that so many people have given so much already. They take some photos and wave good bye before I set off over the Thames to Waterloo station.

Figure 1RNIB HQ

I'm thirsty and want to go into W H Smith for water. I leave my bike at the entrance and go to the nearest till within sight of my bike. You are not supposed to leave the bike unattended so I keep my helmet on so that it's clear to anyone I have left the bike if they look towards the till. That was the plan. Unfortunately, the guy in front of me is taking ages and the people sitting at the shop entrance have left so now my bike has become an item of interest. Two people are standing looking at it. "I'm here" I try to signal. There's only one person ahead of me and they must be finished by now so I decide to wait a few seconds more. When I get outside the folk looking at my bike are displeased and tell me about terrorists and not leaving luggage attended. They are right and I should have asked someone to watch my bike. On a previous trip to London we got told off by the police for taking photos in the station as it could be of use to terrorists. They take things seriously here.

The train is late and the 13:30 turns into the 14:00. However, the 2 bike spaces are free and I get my bike on. I couldn't book the bike onto this train and it was one of my anxiety points as I needed my bike to be in Portsmouth to catch the ferry. The RNIB stop had delayed me a little. Also, I discovered this morning that the ferry requires you to report 45 minutes before sailing or you don't board. This is on page 3 of their web site and not on the ticket. So now all my contingency is gone.

I decide to get off in Portsmouth one stop sooner, as I only have 15 minutes to get to the ferry and I calculate it's a 10-minute cycle. As soon as the train stops I'm off and out the entrance cycling in the direction of the terminal. I decide not to use the cycleway as I'm in a hurry and don't want the winding ways of a cycle path but then find myself on a dual carriageway which isn't pleasant as a number of cars are in the same hurry as me. I'm soon at the gate to the ferry and get ushered up a ramp with 20 other cyclists onto the ferry. Phew. They are all on a trip but have a van to carry their luggage. "70 km a day we do" they tell me. Yes, but without luggage and with a van to sit in I thought. I'm still impressed though because a lot of them look older than me.

I land at Ouistretham in Normandy, a small ferry port and right next to Sword beach where Scottish soldiers came ashore during the D-day landings. I land and then cycle the coastal cycle route to a small village a few miles from the port. I have been told to wait at a sign on the outside of town where Christine will show me to her house. I presume this is a precaution because the single parent, Christine, putting me up, has three daughters. I was worried about staying with a stranger but the greater danger is probably me. I wait by the sign, patiently, as it gets dark but no-one arrives. Christine hasn't been the best communicator and I start to worry. 10 minutes pass and I wonder if she has looked from afar and thought "no thanks". Suddenly she appears and I follow her at pace down some windy streets to arrive at her house. I think she is a little a disappointed as she says "new bike"? My French is not good enough for a conversation and again I think she is disappointed. I'm introduced to her daughter and shown to a play room where there is a mattress on the floor. I hand over the shortbread and finally they are happy. She expected me to have a sleeping bag but I'm happy with a mattress and it's been a long day. She tells me we will have breakfast together at 08:30. I undress and slump on the mattress. Ten minutes later there is a knock at the door and she appears with a blanket which is welcome. I fall asleep as soon as my head hits the mattress. I made it to France.

Figure 2 The bed for shortbread

Day 1 Luc-Sur-Mer 17 miles completed.

CHAPTER 4. CYCLING COMMANDO

I am sleeping on a mattress on the floor of a children's playroom in Luc-Sur-Mer on the Normandy beaches. I wake up to chickens outside my French windows (what else?). They are designer chickens too – a fluffy black one, a normal chicken and a wee nippy black runner chicken. The owner, Christine, is a school teacher and she serves up a wonderful breakfast outside. She tells me about the huge increase in administration in French education and instead of teaching kids she is doing paperwork that never existed before. Sounds familiar. Breakfast is traditional French except I get green menthol tea instead of coffee. Baguette, jam and honey. Christine tells me the chickens lay eggs but not this morning. It's only the eggs the family eat as the children are so used to the chickens they are family pets so they have something else for Christmas. They are easier to keep than dogs as she can leave them for a few days grazing in the garden. I said last night I wanted to leave early in the morning and I think Christine got up early as there is no family breakfast together and her daughters are still asleep. After breakfast, I write in her guest book and say my goodbyes. I want to have time to tour the D-day battlefields. A day later I get an email saying her daughters are enjoying the shortbread.

I start my tour of the Juno and Sword D-day beaches where Canadian, Scottish and British troops landed. The large D-Day beaches are to my right as I cycle west and I wonder what it was like for the soldiers stuck on these beaches. There are sand dunes and ridges to get off the beach and every so often there is a monument to the men who died at this bit of beach or a preserved German concrete pill box. The most amazing monument was the one to the Canadian forces who landed with their bikes. I'm not sure what they were intending to do with their bikes against concrete pill boxes and machine guns. It looked hard to get off the beach and the German fortifications looked formidable.

Many of the names on this coast are Norse in origin and I cycle through villages such as Langrune which in Norse is Land of Green. The Norse men, Vikings, conquered this part of France called Normandy. Normandy then conquered Britain when William the Conqueror landed in 1066. On 6 June 1944 the reverse happened when the Allies landed in Normandy.

My target is Juno beach which is where the Canadian regiments came ashore. The Juno Beach Centre is Canada's Second World War museum and cultural centre located in Normandy, France. The Centre pays homage to the 45,000 Canadians who lost their lives during the War, of which 5,500 were killed during the Battle of Normandy and 359 on D-Day. The centre is both a history of Canada, mixing archive records with Census statistics to better understand the national identity of Canadians and a homage to the war dead. It was opened in 2003 and has a Census/Archives "faces of today" room which explains the diverse make up of Canada today with the history of how that happened. In Canada 5 million people describe themselves as Scottish in origin according to the figures in this room. There are 16 regiments in the Canadian army who are Scottish and wear kilts. Among them are:

The Black Watch (Royal Highland Regiment) of Canada,

The Royal Highland Fusiliers of Canada,

The Lorne Scots (Peel, Dufferin and Halton Regiment).

On D-day itself the Canadian regiments of Scottish origin that landed on the beach were the Cameron Highlanders of Ottawa, the Highland Light Infantry of Canada, the Stormont, Dundas and Glengarry Highlanders, and the North Nova Scotia Highlanders.

One fact that surprised me was the number of Canadians of Ukrainian origin in Canada – 3 million and 30,000 fought for Canada during the second world war.

The staff in the Juno Beach Centre are all Canadians, fluent in both English and French. During the Normandy landings Canadian regiments from French speaking regiments made the landings easier as they could speak to the locals.

Figure 3 Canadian War Memorial

I left the centre and made my way to Sword beach where the British regiments landed. A British cemetery is here at Lion-sur-Mer - a couple of miles inland - and I was struck at the similarity to the cemeteries of the Somme. It is immaculate with every blade of grass cut to a perfect height. Line after line of gravestones – one the many cemeteries holding nearly 18,000 British dead. In the centre of the cemetery there is a white building which has a door and behind this door, is a book showing all graves denoting is buried in the cemetery. Many of the graves are for young men barely 18. One has pebbles on top of the gravestone which is a Jewish custom.

I spoke to quite a few French people in this area who retain a great love for the soldiers that liberated them. I had read before I came that they were resentful of the destruction to their towns and villages but I never heard this opinion once.

A lot of advances for treatment of the blind came from the military after World War 1. In World War 2 1,400 American soldiers were blinded and in the UK the UK Blind Veterans provided assistance. American military doctors needed to rehabilitate these soldiers into society so were at the forefront of innovations to integrate them. In France, the military also innovated - Charles Barbier was an Artillery officer who invented "night writing" so soldiers could communicate at night. The night writing was a series of bumps on paper that could be read by using your fingers. No lights were needed and therefore orders could be passed along the front line without lights giving away positions. Louis Braille in France adapted this night writing for the blind. Dr Armitage of the RNIB then adapted the French Braille for Britain. Each country has their own braille system designed according to their alphabet.

After the cemetery, I visited the Pegasus Bridge that was captured by the British Glider Infantry and gave the Allies a bridge over the river Orne, north of Caen.

My target today was to reach Caen for a late lunch and go to a recommended Vietnamese restaurant. The cycling today had been ok for the first 20 miles but the last 13 were into a headwind and then up hill. My training did not allow for the 32-degree Celsius heat and I'm also now carrying 3 weeks luggage which weighs in at 30lbs. I was pretty exhausted when I arrived in Caen and went straight to the Sa Su Se Vietnamese restaurant that had been recommended. I got there 10 minutes before they closed but they agreed to stay open and I got my first taste of Bo Bun. It is lightly spiced mincemeat with rice noodles, mint, coriander and bean shoots. Very healthy! Food always tastes great after a long cycle. After lunch I didn't stop to take photos in Caen as I just wanted to get up the hill to my hotel. And it was up a hill but eventually I got there. The Hotel Crocus was on a roundabout just next the main Caen War Museum and I presume served the tourist crowd. I didn't bother with the museum as it cost £15 and I had seen a few today.

I fell asleep and didn't wake up till tea time. When I woke up I realised that the whole hotel was a shrine to the Scottish painter Jack Vettriano and every single painting throughout the hotel was by him. They also served wine cheaper than beer so I stayed put, decided to eat in the hotel and planned my next day. It was a couple of miles into town and I did not fancy the long hill climb back to the hotel. While I had a hotel tonight there was nothing booked for the next day. I had to look at the maps on my phone and see what towns were within 20, 30 and 40 miles. Then I checked various accommodation web sites to see what rooms were free. The prices of these hotels mattered. The first day had been really hard for me with the heat, the luggage and my general unfitness. I was anxious about the next day. If there was a head wind or if the route was hilly then I would not be able to cycle much. The heatwave was also a problem as cycling in 32 degrees is not fun.

I worry about all these people sponsoring me – I have said I am cycling to the south of France and now there is pressure on me. Today I only did 33 miles. I did not expect the heat and I did not expect to find it so hard.

I see a town called Clecy on the map and then further on Flers. I need to cycle 40 miles tomorrow so I have to leave myself plenty time. There are not many towns and there is no back-up of a train if I have a problem. I look at the lines but they go east to west and not south. I decide I will get up early and leave at 7 to beat the heat and get some miles under my belt while it is cool. I have to do this.

I went for my tea and ate pizza with a pichet of house wine telling the staff about Jack Vettriano but I'm not sure they were interested. I was sleepy again after the wine and had an early night so I could leave early in the morning. The first day of cycling had been completed and it was nice not sleeping on a floor. End of day 2 - reached Caen - 33 miles completed.

Chapter 5. A bar, a bed and a ballon

I wake up anxious about the day. Yesterday was hard and I have my sponsors watching my daily progress. My dream of cycling effortlessly through the French countryside turned into a slog to make my destination in searing heat. I start the day locked in the hotel, unable to leave. I was ready to depart but couldn't get out the doors through to reception at 6:40. Reception did not open until 7. This was a recurring issue on the trip where French hoteliers lock up the premises in the evening and open up when they get up. Eventually I find a side door that is open but I have nowhere to leave my key as the rest of the hotel was locked tight. I wait till 7 when a cleaner arrives, I hand her my key and then set off to beat the heat.

I follow the cycleway along the river Orne from Caen for a while and then a converted railway line to get to the outskirts. I stop after 90 minutes to eat a chocolate bar and drink water, which is my breakfast. Taking breakfast with me saves on cost. The cycleway ends and I go on minor and not so minor roads. It is Sunday so the main roads are quiet. I am worried about the heat and distance and decide to take the busy roads to get to my destination. Cycleways along riversides are quiet and peaceful but often 30% longer than roads as they snake in their "s" shapes. It is harder cycling as they are not always tarmac. I encounter hill after hill after hill, with my 30lbs of luggage and soon I am walking, walking, walking. This was not what I signed up for and it was a hard morning. Leaving at 7am was a good idea and my thought was that even if I have to walk the last 15 miles I will be at my destination by dark.

Through the day I check the accommodation on my phone and hotel rooms disappear as bookings are made. This is not prime tourist country so there are not a lot of places to stay. My backup plan is warmshowers.org but even they have few places to stay in this area. There is a man emptying the rubbish bins at the layby's and his truck has an open top, flat rear. "I could get my bike on that" I think. However, I decide I can't give up this early and it would feel like cheating. I somehow manage to complete the 38 miles to Flers and sit, exhausted, in a bar in the main square. There is not anything to see here – it is a small town of 15,000 people and a search of Wikipedia tells me nothing interesting happened here. I booked a cheap hotel an hour before and go the short distance to check in and am grateful to lie down on my comfy bed for a quick nap. Today's cycle is exhausting. I sleep for 3 hours and am surprised when I look at my watch. It's nearly tea time again and I venture out to find something open. The hotel is nice and one the main facilities it offers is an ironing room. I have never been in a hotel with an ironing room but there it sits an ironing board with iron in the middle of this room like a modern art exhibition.

It's difficult to find anything open in France on a Sunday. On the outskirts I found a bar – the only one I found open on a Sunday and it's very French. It looks like it has not changed since the 1950's and is empty apart from the couple who run it. He is drinking at his own bar with his wife beside him and they are in their 60s. Its small and an orthopaedic bed sits in the corner with a machine beside it perhaps to help breathing. A commode is next to the bed and toilet paper sits on the bar table. His wife has a stick and she is the bed owner. I suspect they open the bar for the company. The owner is very friendly and spends 5 minutes looking through a pile of newspapers to proudly show me an article about an Englishman who travelled to this area in an old London taxi painted purple. Other people arrive and are told the bar is closed. While walking the high street I noticed a renovated yellow Renault driving up and down just constantly doing that. The driver goes into the bar and is allowed entry. I feel like I'm in a Jean Luc Besson film it's all so surreal. The yellow Renault going up and down, the orthopedic bed in the corner the owner showing me articles from newspapers. I was definitely in France.

Figure 4 Flers and the Renault that goes up and down the high street

The service in La Cantania , a kebab type shop I find open, is really good and the smiling woman does everything she can to make the meal good. I have the Caesar salad although it's Caesar salad unlike anything I have eaten before. It is so hot I do not have an appetite and struggle to eat it.

A "ballon" is a glass of wine in this restaurant. Red in my case. Opposite the restaurant, in a small square, there is a down and out who looks like he has been sleeping rough for months. It's a small town with 15,000 people and they have down and outs. I find that strange.

I get back to my hotel and again plan the next day. What are the potential distances? I figure 30 will be fine and 40 is the optimum. What accommodation is available? Google Maps allows me to see the terrain and I realise the cycling will be the same hilly landscape. Two days in and I am knackered. I try to cheer myself up by telling myself after that it's the Loire valley with riverside riding. If I make the Loire valley it will be easier.

End of day 3 – reached Flers - 38 miles completed.

CHAPTER 6. A CRASH, A SNAKE AND 2 DOGS

I saw two things today that I have never seen in my life - a car crash and a live snake. I was up early again and spread a quarter jar of jam on some baguette to give me energy for the day. The first two days have been exhausting with the distances and heat. I need to watch my money as rural accommodation is more expensive than I expected and €1 for jam on bread saves me €9 for breakfast. I was really pleased as the weather was cooler. The first of the two things I've never seen before happened as I was leaving Flers and sitting at a traffic junction waiting for the lights to turn green. A truck sat to my left, with a van in front of me, as I waited at the lights. Suddenly there was this almighty horn blowing from my left and an object like a Cruise missile from my right traveling at about 40 miles per hour veered across the road and took away the engine of the light van and narrowly missed a head on smash with the lorry. A whisper of spoke came from what was left of the van and there was a strange silence. I took a photo. Not sure why that is my first instinct but I took a photo. The occupants of the car got out and ran from the scene obviously concerned about the smoke. The car driver hugging his female passenger - perhaps in shock. The van driver got out. Everyone was fine. A child of about 6 years old came into view and was crying. I wondered, had the car veered to avoid her? The lights changed to green and I carried on as everyone was fine.

This instinct to photograph is something I've always had. On a previous cycle trip with friends round Avignon, we had found ourselves in Marseille where my friend was getting self-service tickets in the Marseille underground. He was impatient and put his hand in the flap to get the tickets out before they had arrived. His hand jammed and the more he panicked the more the flap dug into his wrist. He started screaming in pain. I lost no time and immediately went into my bag to get my camera out. I took a photo. This was immediately helpful as he started screaming at me and forgot all about his pain. I ran to the ticket office and shouted in my best "allo allo" French with a Scottish accent. The attendant looked at me strangely but then heard the screaming so came out. My friend was shown how to push his hand further into the machine so the flap could be raised and all was fine.

Figure 5 Car Crash in Flers

The cycling today was much better as the weather was cooler and the hills were not as steep.

In France there are many national parks where the wildlife and environment are protected. On this trip I cycled through four and today it is "Parc naturel régional Normandie-Maine". National Parks were invented by a Scotsman called John Muir who grew up in Dunbar. On a cycle trip to Dunbar I visited his museum, the house he grew up in on the High Street. It's a shrine for Americans as John Muir emigrated to America in 1849 made a name for himself exploring that country and eventually established the oldest national park in the world – a place called Yosemite National Park with its Yellowstone geyser. John Muir is better known nowadays and there is a walking trail across central Scotland named after him.

The national parks in France did not get established until a century later from 1968 to 1977. In Scotland our first of two national parks was created in 2002. National Parks are a haven for wildlife as habitation and commercial activities are limited. As I was cycling along I suddenly had to veer seeing a 2-foot-long snake slithering across the forest path. I've never seen a wild snake before and it was the first of a few I encountered. A lot of the cycling today is on old railway lines through forests and in rural areas. The French cycleways are really good and either tarmac or red cinder and today the tracks were straight so I was making good progress.

A little further on in the forest I could see two unaccompanied dogs heading towards me. I'm not a fan of dogs and had a bad experience cycling in Portugal with snarling, barking, wild dogs chasing me on a forest track. My heart was racing as they came toward me and I prepared to sprint for it. They weren't interested. Phew. One had a collar so I expect they were let out for a run.

The weather took a turn for the worse with some rain but I was happy with the cool weather and preferred that to the heat of the sun. My bike and myself were tarred and feathered with the petals from the trees as the rain came lashing down.

This is the first day I've not felt exhausted which I think is down to the cooler weather and the quarter jar of jam I ate. I've been watching my costs, having a "menu du jour" at lunchtime and snacking at night is a good way to do it. TripAdvisor is okay but it only works in areas where tourists go and even then, I never find it that reliable. Generally, I filter on cheap eats in TripAdvisor and there are usually places the local's go listed under that. If you map the cheap eats you then find the area of town to go to for cheap drink and food. Some of the best food I have eaten on past trips has been in the place the locals eat. Today I struck gold and ate the best food of the trip. L'escale is a largish restaurant on the outskirts of Mayenne, my destination for today. I could see lots of tables set-up and staff standing waiting. It was only 11:43 but I had set off at 07:00 and was hungry. I had beer, buffet starter, main course, dessert, coffee and 1 litre of wine for £10. As I sat workmen and local office workers arrived until no table was free. I asked the waitress how much of the wine was mine and she said the drink was unlimited per table. If I finish the wine they bring more!

I couldn't finish the wine nor did I touch the bottle of local cider also on the table. I did sit for two hours and I didn't have an evening meal that day, after the excellent food.

I made my way down to my accommodation which was a room above a pub. I like to try different places to stay and this sounded perfect. I discover that my accommodation is actually in the fortress in one of the oldest areas of town. After dropping off my stuff I did the tourist trail around the town which is very picturesque. The area I am in is near to Orleans and battles with the English are very much part of its history. There is a big Joan of Arc statue outside the main church.

A museum to the "disappeared" is here detailing a dark period in the second world war when many people in Vichy France were deported to concentration camps, including Jews.

As I wander round the battlements of the fortress it rains again. This time it's like a tropical monsoon and something that I'm glad I missed. I return to the bar and think about drafting my blog. I need the password for the Wi-Fi and the owner's wife writes it down. It doesn't work and I go up to the bar and she asks the owner for help. The boss shrugged his shoulders and says "it worked for me" and that's the end of the conversation. I love this

French attitude which I call Parisian. I have been in many areas of France over the years and the attitude of Parisians I find quite different to those of the south.

We used to stay at a hotel in Paris which had an amazing owner. People would arrive and ask the manager if he spoke English and he would say "no" despite being fluent in English. The new arrivals would then struggle to understand everything and he wouldn't answer any questions posed in English. When we arrived, we spoke in our best French and he replied in fluent English. We complained about our room once and he threw us the keys to another room saying "see what you think of this room then". Parisian attitude.

In Mayenne, I go up to my room to get the different Wi-Fi there. I return to the bar in the evening to have a snack of French cheese and some wine. The staff and manager are still working at 10 at night. He is repairing the storm damage to the wind screens outside. I go to bed feeling better after the cooler day.

Day 4 Mon – reached Mayenne - 39 miles completed

An excellent day of cycling along the riverside. Today I do not set off until 08:30 as the weather is cloudy and cool. The last few days in the forest and riverside has been a bit like the Snow White film where all the animals gather round and today is not much different. I saw a snake, 4-foot-long, 4 inches wide, dead by the road side. It was like one of the draft excluders you used to get to sit by doors.

Breakfast in the pub was a French affair with croissant and bread but no plate or napkin. The family who run the pub and accommodation work really hard, up early to take delivery of fresh vegetables and start the days chores. That's after serving until closing time the night before. I thought the owner was sleeping in but he arrived with workmen to continue to repair the storm damage from last night. No warm goodbyes just "leave the key on the hook on your way out". Very Parisian.

As usual I have looked at accommodation and distances with a couple of options for destination. It is a great cycle today along the Mayenne river passing below Chateaux on the hills overlooking the river. I feel a lot more confident on how far I can go now and have started getting in a rhythm. Fueling up in the morning is important and I finished all the jam on the table. I make good time and arrive in Laval. The world-famous milk museum is here and I consider a tour but it's 2 ½ hours and I haven't the time. I'm not sure why being on holiday makes you think you want to visit a milk museum. I don't sit down at night and think "I must look up milk production processes". I suppose being on holiday gives you time to think about things but this is now an adventure not a holiday I stop at the Le Cap Horn - a corner bar under the castle in Laval -order a coke and phone Gordon to update him on progress and hear about his. It is good to speak to him and hear his enthusiasm for the trip, the blog and the JustGiving donations (which are at £900, way past my initial target of £150). The JustGiving web site allows me to keep altering the target so I push it up when we get close to the current target. Each day Gordon's daughter reads out my blog and the JustGiving donations and comments. Gordon gets confused at which blog is which day and cannot follow progress so I change the titles of the blog to say what day, where I am and how far I have cycled.

I carried on out of the historic Laval and was soon getting hungry. I decided I would stop at the next riverside restaurant as I had passed a few, something that was an improvement on the previous days through the forest. I see a restaurant with beer garden, a board with "menu du jour" and people sitting eating. I pull right in take a seat, get brought an English menu and order the ham and potatoes. Five minutes later a brown dish cloth arrives with some food wrapped up inside. I'm confused. I look at the restaurant sign and it says "creperie de moulin". I'm in a creperie. I was hungry so ate it. Can't say I'll ever have another.

The couple in the restaurant had been helpful but spoke only one or two words in English. When I leave I try to take a photo of the dog to show my wife what kind of dog it was. Suddenly the waitress speaks fluent English to me. Amazing. I went through the whole meal with me struggling in French and she never spoke a word. It turns out she came to France from Vietnam 7 years ago to marry a Frenchman. We chatted a while as she described how she struggled to learn French and there is no-one to speak English with. She hates the cold in France. I told her not to come to Scotland.

Figure 6 The dog that started a conversation

I say my goodbye and then 5 minutes later, as I am walking past the houses I say hello to a man who turns out to be a Scotsman from Leith. There are 4 houses at this river lock and he owns 2. It's in the middle of nowhere. He asks me straight off about politics and Brexit. He has just taken French nationality to safeguard his rights and has a dim view of Scotland now, saying people are too obsessed with money. He talks about the twenty years he has spent here and how he can walk into a doctor's surgery and be seen there and then. If he needs an x-ray the doctor sends him to the hospital right away. Apparently Angers nearby has world renowned hand surgeons. I tell him Lothian health board have a Chinese hand expert. His family had owned the grocers in Pitt Street in Leith but he sold up 20 years ago and moved to France. The second house he bought was a shell and he's been renovating it for the last five years. I was hoping he'd invite me in for a cup of tea but no such luck so I say my good-bye's.

I carry on to the town of Chateau-Gontier only to find the last two rooms at my cheap accommodation have gone. I only know where I'll be staying as the day progresses and book the night's stay after lunch. I never know how far I might get and what mechanical problems I may suffer. I don't even have a settled route after Angers as a couple of people have said I should go the inland route instead of the planned coastal one. I scout the surrounding countryside on Google maps and all I can find is a chateau a few miles from Chateau-Gontier at 50% more cost. My options are limited so I decide to go without eating tea to afford the chateau.

When I arrive it's a chateau in its own grounds and I get a double suite. That's two bedrooms with two four poster type beds in a room that's about the size of my house. The owner says I can sleep in either room in the suite. It also has a heated swimming pool which is magic! I have a baguette and a wee bottle of wine which will do me tonight. I appear to be the only guest and I sit in the living room area of my two-roomed suite drinking wine and eating cheese looking out over the estate. I start planning the next day and considering what I do after Angers – west to the coast or east up the Loire valley then south? My money is getting low and I'm thinking of getting a tent for when I get towards the warmer south. I retire to bed early – the exercise, fresh air and wine makes me sleepy.

Day 5, Tue, I reach Chateau-Gontier cycling 43 miles.

A lazy morning waking up in the chateau and having breakfast in the dining room with its chandeliers. The chateau is 18th century and I ask the owner about its history. She bought it 15 years ago and has been working on it ever since, room by room.

I should have taken more photos to let you appreciate her artistry. She has been living her dream she says.

Figure 7 My suite in a chateau

There are many people here living their dream and they all put in many more hours than a "job" – the guy from Leith renovating a property for 10 years, the girl from Vietnam who has spent 7 years away from her family and the couple managing the bar in Mayenne. But they all work 12 hours or more a day.

I expected the cycle to Angers today to be easy but there were a few hills. I had a few phone conversations with close friends and family yesterday. I told my mum that today I would be travelling to the French town of Rangers without the "R". "You're going to Ranges?" she asks. She's not wrong.

Anyway, to the death prevented – I'm cycling along the cycle path and pass a woman with a terrier dog not on a lead. I turn the corner and pass a baby bird sitting in the middle of the cycle track. I avoid it and cycle on but I start thinking "the dog will eat the bird". I stop and turnaround to save the bird from certain death. A life or death decision – I never have to make these at my desk. I'm approaching the bird but so is the dog. I cycle faster. I can't lift the bird as it will then have my smell and be rejected by the mother. The dog is still coming closer. To get the bird to move I shout "shoo" and ring my bell but it just looks up at me. The dog is nearly here and I'm out of options. I turn the wheel towards bird as if to hit it and it jumps up into the air straight into the long grass beside the river. Mission accomplished. It is all so different to sitting at a desk. I cycle on, enjoying the peace and solitude with a sense of satisfaction.

There is lots of wildlife today with some horses, cows and "hairy jennys". No snakes. Check out this website http://www.savonnerie-lait-anesse.fr/ for products from the hairy jennys. I say hairy jenny but it's really a hairy ass. The word donkey replaced ass and a jenny is the name for a she-ass for the same reasons a rooster is no longer called a cock. Language is funny. My spell checker keeps wanting to change "centre" to "center" and "realise" to "realize" and it's the fault of the French. We spoke French for 400 years after 1066 when French speaking William the Conqueror became king and gave all his French speaking pals castles and land, including Robert de Brus (Robert the Bruce). When printing started we used the letters that sounded like the words and used "realize" and "center". The British that went to

America used that English spelling which the Americans still use today. In about 1800 the British decided they would change English spelling to match the country of origin of English words. So "Center" became "centre" which makes no sense and it's "programme" not "program" and all words of French origin ending in "ization" went with the French "s". My "allo allo" French works because many words are the same and it's just the "prononciation" (that's the French spelling of pronunciation). Forty per cent of the English language is French. Magnifique!

In France all the churches let you know the bars are open by ringing their bell 12 times. Right after this announcement I come across a river ferry with a bar on the other side. The ferryman uses ropes to pull us across to the Ile Rubin where I enjoy a beer overlooking the river.

I misjudge the distance today as the cycle route is not the same as crow flies as I am following the river Mayenne which flows into the Maine in Angers (Rangers without the "R"). I cross the river and head up to my restaurant of choice, le Saigon, another Vietnamese place which closes at 2. I then make my way to the accommodation for tonight opposite the university of Angers.

Angers is a very big, ancient town with lots of narrow cobbled streets and has an abundance of Americans. The big castle d'Angers was never taken in siege and is where the Duke of Wellington got his military training before the battle of Waterloo. The castle has the biggest and oldest collection of medieval tapestries in the world so I take a look. Pretty amazing. It depicts the apocalypse and was completed in 1384. It is like the world's largest comic book with 90 tapestry panels and tells the story of the final battle between good and evil.

When you first go in to see them there are a couple hanging on a wall in an air-conditioned room. You turn a corner and it's like an aircraft hangar and I audibly went "wow".

Figure 8 The biggest tapestry in the world, Angers

The final panels have a prostitute riding a dragon against Satan and the forces of good win. I wander the castle walls after this, looking at the gardens on top of the walls. The battlements are 13 to 15 feet thick and have gardens at the top growing herbs and vegetables, as a university experiment using the same vegetables they used in medieval times. Apricots are a favourite of this area and many local dishes have the fruit included.

After a consultation with the tourist office I decide to change my route. The best route is up the Loire valley to the east to Saumur then south to Thouars, Niort and West to La Rochelle I am told. So, my planning for the next couple of days goes out the window and I plan a new route.

I need to wait till 5pm for "after work" prices in the bars when you get half price beer, but it is not long till the magic hour arrives. On the way to the bar I meet another person living their dream. Anton loves bikes and books so he opened a shop selling both. Why not?

I sit in the Tonton Fuch street side bar on the main road of Angers drinking my happy hour beers at €3 a pint watching the world go by and updating my blog. I plan my routes three days in advance as there is no good heading in a direction only to find on day three the distances are too long or there is no accommodation. I plot all towns within 100 miles and draw lines between them showing distances. This allows me to understand the various possible routes and I add accommodation prices, availability, and in some cases hills.

I stay at the university d'Angers tonight in a little apartment where I microwave my lasagna bought from the supermarket downstairs. It wasn't very good but it saved some money.

Day 6, Wed, I reach Angers 38 miles completed.

Figure 9 The route for the first 8 days

So far, I have travelled south to the Loire river through

Ouistratam
Caen
Flers
Mayenne
Chateau-Gontiers
Angers

and completed nearly 300km. It has been very hard and things are about to get worse.

Chapter 9. A slag, a near drowning and I lose my passport

I wake up knackered this morning with no energy. Had 1/4 jar of jam, a mars bar, carrot cake and sweet hot chocolate but just could not get my energy levels up. This is the seventh day cycling each day carrying my 30lbs of luggage to a new place. I think I need a rest day. The forecast for tomorrow is violent thunderstorms with hailstones. I read a few days ago that 1000 people were killed in a freak hailstorm near here so everything points to a day in doors and a chance to do a washing. The hailstones event happened 500 years ago but with my luck you never know. Cycling at home with my clothes was fine but in the 27-degree heat today it's not working. I have sores on my lips, sores that mean I can't sit on my saddle and the 4-year-old sun cream doesn't work. I need a holiday.

I decided yesterday that I was going east inland up the Loire valley instead of west to the coast. All the advice I have had so far is that it's nicer this way and looking at the size of the towns it is a better bet for accommodation. I'm not in the mood for camping yet and the warmshowers.org is a bit too stressful - staying for free in someone's house means you can't just relax. After an exhausting day on the bike I'm not in the mood for polite conversation with strangers. It is some years since I camped and I can no longer get through the night without a trudge to the toilet block. But my money is getting eaten up and I decide when I am closer to the end I will economise. The route out of Angers takes me past the industrial ruins of old mine pits. A huge slag heap is planted with trees and all around there is shale and lakes of stagnant water. Old mine heads sit silent. I follow the cycle path through this barren landscape passing various art works along the way until I come to a river. The path heads directly to the river and I can see it continuing on the other side. I'm confused.

I check the map on my phone and the bike path goes right across the river where I'm standing. I see a platform boat the length of 2 bikes with a chain that goes under the water. I must have to put the bike on and pull the boat across by the chain. I don't like the look of the water or the width of the river. The fact that I am alone and I'm unclear as to the physical effort required worries me. I gently run the bike down the 45-degree concrete ramp, put one foot and one wheel on the boat and it sets off. The other foot is on land and I'm straddled between land and boat. The water is pure brown and looks deep. I manage to grab the chain and pull the boat back. I hold the chain while getting the bike on. Now I have to pull the boat across the river. It's only me and it was hard work - I would guess my bike and luggage weigh 25kg plus. I get to the other side determined not to repeat mistakes but as I have reeled in the chain I've wrapped it round my ankle. As I go to step off my leg won't move, the bike veers to the side and one of the two clasps holding my bag on the bike snaps off. The boat starts to move away from the ramp and the bike looks like it's going under water with the bag still hanging by one clasp. I grab the chain again and pull the boat back towards the concrete ramp. I then jump, with my bike, gaining minor scratches along with the bike that I drag up the concrete ramp. I feel like I've been in an episode of Dads Army.

Figure 10 Bike ferry with steep 45-degree incline from bank

I cycle on. The route isn't particularly tough but I'm very weary.
It's hot again and not even 11 o'clock. I stop for carrot cake and
coffee adding two sachets of sugar hoping it will get me going. I
look for accommodation on Airbnb and decide I definitely need
a rest day. I need to do a washing too. My friend gets four days
out of his underpants - front, back to front inside out and inside
out back to front. It's a joke but based on truth judging by the
picture of his pants that went around by email. That picture is
now used by diet plan companies. My other issue is I am wearing
Scottish cycle clothes – not lycra but shorts made for the cool
Scottish summer and not the furnace I'm cycling in today. I apply
to book a 400-year-old house through Airbnb in the old town
of Saumur. I like to stay somewhere different every night but
it says that I have to wait 24 hours for a reply. I need it tonight.
This place has a washing machine. I am so tired I now cycle on
the busy road instead of the cycle path which winds and has a
poor surface. I try to get out of the burning sun by stopping in
a bus shelter and drinking water. I see an advert for the "Musée

des Blindés" in Saumur. How weird is that – a museum for blind people on this trip raising money for blind people. I check my map for a Decathlon and there is one on the outskirts of town that I will pass where I can buy better cooler clothes. Eventually I get to the outskirts of Saumur and head for the McDonalds for air conditioning, Wi-Fi and energy drinks. I end up sitting for three hours trying to recover. A coke a burger and chips costs more than the lunch a few days ago with unlimited wine. I get a coffee and its cold so I complain and they bring another. No coffee comes out the spout. They had put two lids on. "We play a joke" the waitress says laughing. The new coffee is still cold. I don't laugh. An hour of that time I chat to Gordon – I have a lot to tell him with the boat and all. I get a reply about my accommodation and I can stay there tonight so that is good. The man who rents the house in the old town says he can't be there till 7 so I have plenty time to enjoy the cool air in McDonalds.

It is very important to keep your valuables safe and also to have backup. I have my valuables in three locations. Credit card and day money in my trouser pocket, a small lightweight bag with wallet, passport, spare glasses, hearing aid batteries and a third emergency stash in my pannier bag. That way if I lose one bag I still have the other two.

Decathlon is across the road and I go and get the clothes I need. That goes well and I get a cheap sleeping bag for later if I use WarmShowers or get caught between towns and have to sleep outside.

Time for a beer and I head into the centre of town. When I get to the tourist office I go to my pannier bag to get my valuables bag with passport wallet etc. and it's not there. It's not in the other pannier bag either. I rush into the tourist centre and ask them to phone Decathlon. I must have left it in the changing room. After an age Decathlon tells the woman in the tourist office that there is nothing there. I cycle straight to Decathlon with an energy I never had all day, run into the store and the changing room I used is empty. The girl on the customer desk says nothing has been found. I've lost my wallet, passport, bank cards money, tablet and charger for phone. The end of a perfect day.

CHAPTER 10. THE BAG OF VALUABLES LOST

I have two backups for money as this isn't the first holiday with issues. I have history. Over the years I have organized over 30 cycle trips for friends in just about every country in western Europe. We toured various cities and towns throughout Europe and the potential for losing things was 5 nights in 5 hotels times 6 cyclists. I like to be prepared for problems then if they happen it isn't a problem. For each trip, we have a sheet of paper with contact numbers, passport numbers, medication and other details. I have a spare credit card stashed away some cash hidden elsewhere and take a spare smart phone as usually, as trip leader, all the maps and navigation is done by my phone. The first trip wasn't actually a cycle trip but a cheap flight to Paris where 4 of us stayed in the Pigalle area near the Moulin Rouge. This was in January 2002 and the early days of Ryanair in Scotland that required a 4 am start and a cross country trip to Prestwick airport. The hotel we stayed in was on the main boulevard in the "red light" district which in Europe is an area full of shops, houses and restaurants. Anyway, one evening we got back to the hotel and one of our rooms had been broken into. Gordon was in the room with another friend. We had to go up to the police station and report the theft so we could then go to the embassy and get a replacement passport. The police station was a fortress, with armed police at the entrance and a series of wire mesh fences to go through. The police interview Gordon's room mate who gives details of the passport, gloves, hat and other clothes that were stolen. The interviewer diligently writes down the long list of things taken and then turns to Gordon "Monsieur Gordon, please list for me the things you had stolen". Gordon hesitates and then says "nothing". The room had been ransacked but the thieves didn't fancy any of Gordon's stuff and it was all left. After that incident, I prepared for the worst in all future trips and dressed like Gordon.

Even further back in my life, at school around 1978, I would tour Europe with friends hitching, eurorailing or cycling. The hostels in those days were quite often in red light districts as that was where they could get cheap dormitory property. I remember cycling to Brussels Youth hostel aged 18 and all the brothels in the same street with balconies that the girls stood on. They all whistled and shouted at four 18-year-old naive Scots who had packed their paisley-pattern pyjamas for a trip round Europe. Kids ran out from these houses trying to take the bicycle pumps off our bikes until we got to the fortress security of the hostel. On my second trip round Europe in 1980 I would wear old clothes an old watch and generally look as if I didn't have money so as not to attract attention. Gordon had shown me how to perfect that in Paris with thieves not taking anything. My worst loss was, as mentioned earlier, in remote Cuba, cycling in similar heats to this trip and I lost my passport, glasses, hearing aid batteries, wallet, money, credit cards, driving license, exit visa and everything that would enable me to see and hear for the rest of the trip

So, I have history. On this trip I had a strategy of two money backups, cheap clothes and no watch. I knew I could ring ahead to the consulate in Bordeaux or embassy in Paris and they could issue a temporary passport in a morning. I now needed to phone the police and ask Decathlon for any CCTV. I hadn't trusted the staff to go to the right changing place but sure enough it had been empty when I checked. I made out a description of the bag. The uniform security staff arrive. As I speak to the staff I see a grey bag sitting on the table in the security room. They had found it but not told any store staff. I was so, so pleased. The guard wouldn't let me have it though. I had to show him my passport photo and driving license from the wallet. I gave him €10 for a beer and got a wee bunch of flowers for the tourist woman. Oh, happy days.

After I get my valuables I set off for my Airbnb accommodation in Saumur. It's in the oldest area of town up cobbled streets and I soon meet Frederique who shows me my ground floor apartment. It looks 16th century and while quite basic has a certain charm. The washing machine is a top loader with huge jaws to open that resemble the teeth of a great white shark. Too late to do a washing so I wander down to the end of the street where there is a 17th century square. Tables are set up and a jazz band is playing. The local wine producer at Chateau de Targe is giving away free wine all evening and putting on the music. Woohoo as I suddenly develop a deep interest in the many varieties of wine on offer. No red but on a hot night like tonight the many varieties of Rose are welcome. I wander over to a creperie that sells cheap red and order an omelette as the brown dish cloth does nothing for me. I sleep well that night.

Day 7, Thu, Saumur 36 miles completed.

In the morning, I have a lazy lie in. I really need this rest. Sitting at a desk all week is really not good and I was pretty unprepared for the physical effort and heat exhaustion. I never pretended to be an athlete. I really like the top loader washing machine as you can see how much is in the drum. It took a bit of understanding, especially to open the shark jaws to put your clothes in but I manage and soon I will have clean fresh clothes. The rain forecast is for 2pm so I need to get my clothes dry and stick them on a clothes horse out in the narrow cobblestone street. This causes some amusement and some irritation to the car drivers who have to navigate past the horse.

I decide to go for a pizza lunch to save money and find one recommended in TripAdvisor. It was terrible. After lunch I bring in my washing and decide to go to the "Musée des Blindés" which is actually the largest tank museum in the world. "Blindes "in English means "armour". It's a huge place over a number of aircraft hangers with over 800 armoured vehicles from every age and every country around the world. There is a show on the next day and tank engineers are revving up the tanks and driving them round the car park. A couple of folk run out and move their cars as some of the tank drivers do not appear experienced with little steering or clutch control.

Figure 11 Four of the 800 tanks in the Musée des Blindés

On the way back to the house I buy nappy cream for my sores. I have stayed off the bike all day but I am concerned for tomorrow. When I get home it's more cheese and wine and an early bed. It never rained but it's now scheduled for tomorrow when I'm cycling. The best news is a drop of 8 degrees in temperature for the next few days. 22 max.

CHAPTER 11. READING THE TOILET BOWL

I used to teach English to newly arrived communist Chinese people who had no experience in Western culture. They also gave me tips from their culture and would insist that each morning I should look into the toilet bowl and all would be revealed. The Chinese culture is 3000 years old so it's something to respect. So, this morning after ablutions I peer into the bowl, apply the Chinese interpretation and confirm the day is looking good.

I return to my bedroom to find a brown sticky substance on the floor and my pannier bag. Why I was carrying chocolate in this weather is a mystery. I had to wash the floor and my pannier and discard the chocolate. I woke at 5 a.m. today determined to set off at first light and also to miss the storm that had thoughtfully delayed its arrival by 24 hours. By 11 am it was to be torrential rain, hailstones and wind. I was ready to go and was to hide the house keys in the communal electricity cupboard in the stair hallway. As I put the key in the place instructed there was a BANG and a green flash. It appeared I had disturbed the electrical cables with the metal key and I had heard a fuse box switch drop. Which flat was now without electricity I could not tell as there was a fuse box for each flat. It was 6:20 am and not a time to play around with fuse boxes. I reasoned that whoever had the problem would come downstairs and reset their fuse box.

So, I was off. I was pretty anxious when I woke up as the exhaustion from two days before had not been pleasant. However, I now had my travelling chemist shop of sun tan lotion, ibuprofen, nappy rash cream and hydration tablets. The sores on my lips had calmed down and the saddle sores had recovered. I had my new lightweight shorts on and the weather was cool. I decided to take roads rather than the cycle track. It's a constant battle to find cheap available accommodation in this part of France and I often have to go a longer way to find somewhere. Today, when setting off in the morning, I don't know where I'm staying tonight and only when I'm within touching distance will I book. Today I'm cycling uphill all day and trying to cycle the usual couple of hours before I stop for some breakfast. I'm now leaving my second national park - the Loire-Anjou-Touraine Natural Regional Park - and take a number of back roads through the forest. There are small clearings every so often and shacks that look lived in. Whether it's for day time or full time use I can't tell. I'm cycling through remote areas alone and I'm glad it's early in the morning. A forest is perfect cover should someone decide to rob me! I make good time and the uphill is gentler than I expected. I leave the forest after an hour and now cycle across rolling grasslands and fields sticking to tarmac. Sometimes the roads turn to gravel but the map doesn't tell me this. Gravel means punctures so I'll go a longer route if necessary and sometimes turn back to find tarmac. My bike is new and I have never repaired a puncture. Also, the wheels are security locked, needing a special key to get off and I really do not want the hassle. The last bike I had was taken apart and put together several times as I had it for 17 years. Triggers bike I called it. Everything on the bike had been replaced at one time or another and only the frame was the same.

I cycle 36 miles uphill in 5 hours but with no major climbs. Today is cooler and the roads are tarmac. When I stop for breakfast I realise I have left it on the bunker of the last house. Sigh. A mars bar substituted.

When I arrive in Airvault, my destination, the Saturday market was on and the locals were all out.

There is a busy wee coffee shop on the square and I stop for a coffee. Quite a few folk chat to me and eventually I meet the mayor (allegedly) who explains the cafe is raising money for sick kids and before long I am making a donation and having my photo taken. Then I end up playing speed chess with the locals. They all play a similar style and are used to each other's play. I win the first game and we draw a crowd. The next game I lose in 5 minutes. Played a few, win some lose some and they ask if I will be back next week. Tempting, but no. I go for something to eat after this and found one of the best restaurants on the trip for quality but perhaps not for price. Again, I chose from the "plat du Jour" with some beautiful sea bass.

I wander round this ancient town while waiting for my digs to open and get chatting to the tour guide at the church. She is an art student graduate who had been employed by the mayor (whose photo was nothing like the guy raising money for sick children). We are talking about art (or rather the three things I had seen on my tours including The Last Supper fresco mural in Milan) and it was an enjoyable hour. She offered me a free tour of the underground fountain and caves as she had the keys. Not for the claustrophobic. She insisted I go down some tunnel to the source of the water and it was a squeeze at 4 feet high. I wasn't sure how far we were going and started not to like the journey down the incline while bent over but it was only a minute and we were at the chamber. Great to get the tour and she proudly showed me the trickle of water coming out the rock. The church and town were a stopover for the pilgrimage to Santiago de Compostella a town in the west of Spain reputed to have the bones of St James buried in the cathedral. Pilgrims drank rom the fountain and stayed overnight.

I still had an hour to go and the girl suggested I visit France's biggest hat museum. It was free and I spent a long 15 minutes looking at the hundreds of hats in three buildings. They have some weird museums here.

The accommodation tonight in Airvault was run by an Englishman called Mark. Quite possibly the most welcoming place I have been to. A free beer was presented to me on arrival, always a good start. The promised torrential rain has arrived, and it's freezing. Thank goodness I'm in doors and head up for a shower then update my blog.

When I come downstairs I meet 8 Dutch male and female pensioners who spend 4 months cycling each summer. One of the women drives a van with their luggage and they have cycled from the south of Spain. A support van sounds good. My anxiety levels about the cycling have gone down perhaps because it is cooler. I know if I get up early then I can make it. I check the route and tomorrow is a big cycle but it is difficult to see how it can be avoided. It will be another early start tomorrow.

Mark gives me a plate and a bottle of wine from his cellar at suppertime and I snack before heading to bed.

Day 9, Sat, Airvault 36 miles completed.

I leave my accommodation in Airvault at 8 a.m. in an attempt
to cycle 45 miles today. The weather is 8 degrees cooler and it
makes a huge difference. Still hard going as 45 miles is the same
distance as Edinburgh to Glasgow. I weighed my luggage this
morning and it weighs 30lbs. I wonder what I weigh?

Have you ever met a rich hotelier? The Englishman running
the hotel in Airvault works till midnight and is up at 6 a.m. We
chatted quite a lot about various things and in the morning, he
waives my bar bill when I check out. A not insignificant gesture
given my alcohol consumption. I snake out of Airvault on a quiet
country road still wet from yesterday's rain.

The 45 miles on my route include quite a few hills and wrong
turnings but I complete them without much incident. I take a
wrong turning in Parthenay as the French have this habit of
numbering different roads with the same number and at odd
angles so you can easily end up turning the wrong way. I arrive in
the town of Niort at 2 p.m. The days are definitely getting better
when I sum it up in a couple of sentence like that! Six hours of
riding and just one sentence. My fitness training is on the job but
I definitely feel more confident now. The cool weather and the
early start, late lunch, rhythm I have is working well. I booked
into the Hotel de France, a boutique place in the centre of the
shopping area of Niort. This is another French town with history
and the castle in Niort was built for William the Conqueror.
Quick history – William, Duke of Normandy and vassal of the
King of France invaded England in 1066 and declared himself
king of England which then meant the King of England was the
vassal of the King of France. This caused trouble later. French
was the language of England until 1425. I remember from school
being taught "Gardez lieu" was shouted in Edinburgh when

rubbish was thrown out the window. Edward II rebelled against the French king and King David II of Scotland invaded England to help the French who had lost the battle of Crecy. Then there was the 100 years' war. So, England, France and Scotland have been intertwined for 100's of years.

Sundays in France mean everything is closed – shops and restaurants. It seems hard to believe that it is a week since the night in Flers with the orthopaedic bed. The evening was therefore spent in a kebab shop at the station and it was interesting watching the various characters. The guy running the shop was known to everybody and at one point was shouting "I love you" to a woman at a window across the road. Another woman poorly dressed, came in and countersigned a printed cheque to get alcohol. She could barely stand and was about 40. My evening was finished in a bar in the main square next to the Nessie figures found throughout the town.

Day 10, Sun, Niort 45 miles completed.

Chapter 13. I lose my credit card

As I have said, nothing on this trip is pre-booked as I make it up as I go along. Each night I have to plan the next day or two – accommodation available, prices, weather conditions, prevailing wind, back-up plan, hills, road surface and bike friendly roads. I write on a bit of paper all the towns within 100 miles and then plan the distances between them. If I feel bad then I have a town not too far away that I can stop at. If things go well I can travel further. Accommodation available the night before can disappear in the morning. Accommodation available in the morning can disappear by lunchtime. So, I have to check the internet regularly. I don't want to book the accommodation until lunchtime as I am never sure how far I will get.

The day in Saumur I was exhausted I could hardly move and I retain an anxiety that it happens again. Twenty miles on a poor surface uphill into a headwind in the heat is much more exhausting than fifty miles on a flat tarmac with the wind behind you. The heat is the enemy.

The heat exhaustion has happened to me before and a coke saved my life. We had been cycling up unexpectedly steep hills in Spain ten years ago. It was extremely hot so I became dehydrated and my blood sugar levels were very low. I felt faint, could get no energy at all and could barely move. Marathon runners call it the knock. I had to sit down under a tree in the shade and sip water but it made no difference. I felt so bad I wanted to go home although I wasn't sure how I would get the energy to go home. My friend suggested I have a coke instead of water. Normally I do not drink fizzy juice but I would have drunk sheep's urine if I thought I would have felt better. So, I drank the coke and 10 minutes later I was a new man. The sugar and caffeine boosted my system and I was back to normal. Difficult to describe in writing the feeling of heat exhaustion. The rest of that trip there was always a coke and a mars bar in my pannier.

Today strong head winds were forecast, then rain. There was no route that I liked with headwinds and hills so I contemplated taking a train. One of my sponsors specifically said I could not take a train as that would be cheating. Going west by train is not cheating, I told myself, as it's not taking off mileage and a lateral transfer. I don't need to put it in the blog and I wouldn't lie if someone asked but neither will I announce it. Tour de France riders do transfers so what's the problem? When I started the trip a train was always the option as I was on holiday so no problem. I'll get the train and not say. I check the timetables and route.

I have a voice that talks in my ear sometimes. I read up on it and it's called a conscience. A little angel in one ear and the devil cherub at the other. "Take the train Andy" "No-one will mind" says the devil cherub. "You'll be the man who cycled France except for the train journey" says the angel. I check the JustGiving page for the text of the sponsor that feeds the angel. "North to South, top to bottom, up to down - they all feel downhill to me. Feet up and let it roll. No trains now. Stay safe" Argh. No. It says "no trains now" Quite specific, that's the contract and I can't break it. I check the railway line and a third of the way there is a station. So, I plan to cycle and if it's really bad I have an out. But I have to cycle.

I was up early and out at 7:30 am and left the Hotel de France in Niort cycling through the empty winding alleyways out of town. I'm glad I listened to the angel as it's less windy in the morning. The JustGiving page is showing £1405 with generosity shown by so many. Every second day I phone Gordon who closely follows each day's events on the blog. He is now able to follow my trip as the blog titles have been changed to be more helpful to someone with no sight. It was a stupid error as I used to be in charge of the web team at my work and building in accessibility is a fundamental. The blog posts are in chronological order so the latest appears at the top of the page but a person with no sight cannot easily understand that. I retitled the posts so far with "Day 1", "Day 2" etc. and the name of where I am. When Gordon gets the post read out to him he now knows which day and what town so in his head he can understand the context and sequence.

It turns into a really good day and thoughts of a train disappear. Three in a row, good cycles after my day's rest and I feel more confident. I get to Surgeres the last town with a railway station before the railway line veers away from my cycle route and decide to stop for breakfast. Surgeres has a population of 6,000 but it is here I find the friendliest bar in France. The owner and his wife both came over to say "bonjour". The staff were really nice and quite a few people were having beers at 10:30 making a great atmosphere and I like that, despite the time. They didn't serve food when I asked but suggested I go to the boulangerie, get what I want and bring it back. I knocked over some guys coat, go to pick it up then couldn't find my just bought choc au pain, only to realise I had laid my valuables bag on it. Pancake au pain now. The barmaids work hard and fast, smile and exchange pleasantries with customers who come and go. I suddenly realise that the music playing is the play list from my phone and the last two songs are mine "Rock the Casbah" and "Sweet Dreams". The third song starts and it's "a Town called Malice". I check my phone. It might be broadcasting but it isn't. All three songs were released in 1982 and it's a CD of the year. Great music, great company and I contemplate a beer. But I need to get on. "No trains" said my sponsor and rain and wind is still forecast.

I leave the bar and instead of heading off I linger to take photos of the best bar in France. The barmaid comes running out as I take the photo. "Monsieur, monsieur. Votre carte de credit" I had dropped the credit card in the bar. Second escape. Again, I have previous here and the card is kept in the pocket that is never used except this time it was.

Figure 12 Barmaid running out with my credit card

I cycle on and dark heavy clouds hang over-head keeping it cool. The head wind gets up but doesn't affect me as much as I feared as the road snakes meaning the headwind is not often fully in my face. The storm kept promising to arrive all afternoon but never did. The cycling was good today on minor tarmac roads through farmland and then a huge irrigated area – "marais" in French – with more waterways than roads.

I get to Rochefort in good time thinking I would enjoy the cheese of the same name and was disappointed to find that the name of the cheese is actually Roquefort. The main attraction here is a replica of the 1770 frigate "Hermione" which fought against the British in the American War of Independence. Photo opportunity but I was disappointed to find the RNIB shirt still didn't fit me despite 11 days on the road. I expected to be slimmer. I discover I've been wearing it back to front as the writing should be on the back. I'm not coming out looking very good on my blog.

Lunch is Vietnamese again but I never tire of it. The wine here is even cheaper and the food the usual excellent fare. I head out of town to the outskirts, to my budget hotel, IBIS. There are 5 French people in their 60's having a picnic at a table outside having moved the one table into the sun. They remind me of my aunt and uncle. I ask inside if I can take a chair out for the woman who looks like my aunt and I make instant friends. There is not much around as I'm in the outskirts and the cycle into town is not attractive so I visit the local supermarket for the cheese I hoped to get here, bread and wine. It's nearly impossible to find a screw top bottle of wine in France so I have to take a cork one. On return to the hotel I ask for a corkscrew but they don't have one. I'm in France, it's a hotel and they don't have a corkscrew. They suggest I go to a local restaurant and they will open it for me. I don't fancy that and remember I have this multitool thing in my cycle kit. I check all 16 devices and there is no corkscrew. Reluctantly, I set off for the local restaurant and pass the picnickers. Aha – they have wine open, so I ask for the corkscrew. Success.

I sit in the sun then retire to my room for Roquefort, bread and wine. Day 11, Mon, Rochefort 45 miles completed.

Chapter 14. The world's most terrifying bridge

A very windy day and to beat the heat I'm up at 5:30am. The French tell me it's really cold and the last 4 days have been 10 degrees cooler than the first week.

Today I have to negotiate the marshlands and get across the river at Rochefort. They have a gondola bridge which I didn't know existed as I thought the Vizcaya gondola bridge in Bilbao was unique. I love gondola bridges. It's two cranes joined up making a "n" shape over the river. A platform big enough for four cars is suspended from the crane and then swung across the river on chains. This is the gondola.

Leaving the IBIS budget hotel, I have to take a ring road that turns out to be a dual carriageway where lorries pass very close. This unnerves me as they are very noisy, fast and the slip stream catches me when they pass shoogling the bike. I was pleased to be going across the quieter gondola bridge for cars but when I got there I found it was closed for three years for renovation. No matter I thought as I will take the ferry. However, the sign says it does not open till 9 and is closed on a Tuesday. I look at the bridge with the lorries and it's very high and it's very windy. I look at the river and the wind makes it very choppy for a ferry crossing. It's only 07.30 a.m. so a long wait for the ferry but I decide I'd rather do that, then be on the same road as the juggernauts. Wait! I remember today is Tuesday! The ferry sign says closed Tuesday so the bridge it has to be. A Frenchman sees my face and stops to ask if I am lost. I explain my dilemma but he tells me not to worry as there is a cycleway on the high bridge. The dual carriageway to the bridge is busy but right enough when I get to the bridge there is a line of white paint to protect the cyclists. A line of white paint! I'm surprised because in other parts of France cyclists are separated from traffic by a kerb, a hedge or raised bull bars. The bridge is a steep climb – its tall for ships to pass underneath and it looks like a budget bridge that somebody saved money on. The traffic lanes are narrow and the lorries must keep on the inside lane so they stray into the cycle lane. Lorries travelling at 80kmh passing very close to me and they are not expecting a bike. The wind howls from my right side threatening to blow me over into the path of the lorries. The noise of the juggernauts hurtling past me, so close on my left is deafening. I have been in heavy traffic before but this is dangerous as the lorries are going into the cycle lane. One passes so close halfway into the cycle lane that I feel the lorry behind him is going to hit me. The lorry behind has no idea I am there and will be in the cycle lane the same as the others, probably doing the same as me keeping to the right trying to stop the wind buffeting him from the left. My nerve breaks. I can't do this anymore and I climb onto the narrow ledge beside the crash barriers. I shuffle along this ledge with my bike maybe 8 inches wide and full of overgrown weeds. My leg hits the pedals again and again as there is not enough space to walk beside the bike. I am slightly behind it, shuffling baby steps like a childhood game. The lorries still roar past, the wind from their slipstream and the gale from my right, at the summit of the bridge. The crash-barrier is below my waist height so I keep the bike between me and the barrier so I do not get blown off the bridge into the river. Shuffle, shuffle, my ankle hits the pedal, ow, shuffle, shuffle, ROAR of juggernauts always in twos, shuffle, shuffle, big weed, shuffle. Thirty minutes of this and I am off the bridge.

Figure 13 The worlds most terrifying bridge

At this point I decide there is no way I can take the road I planned
with all the lorries and decide to add 14 miles to my journey
by heading north west then south east. The other days on main
roads had been Sunday's and early mornings. I had thought that
being in this out of the way, western part of France, with no
major towns, I would be on a quiet road but today I am not lucky.
I decide I'd rather cycle till midnight than risk this road and set
off across the marshlands. It's a long slog crisscrossing a canal
network while the gale blows, sometimes into my face. Lots
of animals here, grazing on little islands with no possibility of
escape. I wonder how they get there across the canals. It is here I
see the biggest roadside death with a dead swan, it's huge wings
spread-eagled like a crucifixion. I wonder what killed it as I am
cycling on a single track minor road. I carry on and see another

cyclist in the distance whom I catch up on. I say "bonjour" and after some poor French from me he switches to English. His name is Giles, he's 75 years old and fitter than me. He is also cycling from the north to the south of France but started in Brittany rather than Normandy. He worked as a doctor for Medicines Sans Frontiers and has been to every disaster area or war zone you could mention and we cycle for a while swapping stories. Mind you the only disaster areas I can describe are my cycle trips. Giles looks like Jon Pertwee in Worzel Gummidge and, at 75, is probably the same age. I cycle on ahead as I have to catch another ferry across the Gironde a wide channel of water that takes 40 minutes to cross by ferry. The trees and animal life has changed from the snake forests earlier in the trip. Now there are huge dragonflies, insects that buzz loudly in my ear and, lizards scuttling away, pine trees and palms. Two days and 100 miles ago it was quite different.

I stop for a coke in the small town of Marennes just before I come to another bridge. I probably need a vodka to go with it if it's going to be like the last bridge. While checking my phone I discover that hackers appear to have targeted me. In France, you are giving your details to small hotel IT systems. I have read before that they are notoriously insecure using old software and computers making them a prime target for hackers. Anyway, I find a £10 payment on my credit card to PayPal which wasn't me, so I phone the bank and they can't find anything that explains the payment. I don't want to cancel the card so they suggest waiting. Next morning, I get an email from PayPal saying they have noticed strange activity and ask me to check all purchases are genuine. This is interesting as I don't have a PayPal account active. The email is a scam – it looks genuine but the link to PayPal takes you elsewhere so they can get your username and password. This is the only day I get such an email and never have I got one since so I am pretty sure someone was trying to hack me. The charge on my credit card has never been explained and the statement said no more.

I leave Marenne and make my way towards the bridge. A huge cloud saltire appears in the sky above me and the bridge and I quickly take a selfie as evidence. A white cross on a blue background, the cross of St Andrews the national flag of Scotland. The last time this happened the Scots were battling the English in 892 AD and the appearance of a cross in the sky spurred them onto victory. This happened in Athelstaneford, East Lothian where today there is a museum to the flag. My luck may now be changing and today I will perhaps cycle to victory – but first the bridge.

Figure 14 Saltire appears in the sky top right

When I get to it, it is not as steep as the last one and it has a kerb between the cyclists and the road which is a single track. No thundering lorries traveling at speed and a nice gentle ride, if rather windy, across this bridge. The cross has brought me luck after all. I arrive in La Palmyre on the Gironde estuary at lunchtime and realise I have missed my ferry but they are every 90 minutes so I enjoy a relaxing lunch. There are many seaside resorts here but their season must be very short as half the restaurants are shut and the ones open are not busy with one or two people sitting in a sea of empty tables. I find one, out the way, that is busy – a good sign – and sit at the last free table. After lunch the journey to Royan, where I catch the ferry, is pleasant along a seafront of houses for the last few miles. I pass a monument to British commandos who travelled from Scotland by submarine to canoe up the Gironde and raid Bordeaux in World War 2. They shortened the war by 6 months according to Winston Churchill and you can find a documentary narrated by Paddy Ashdown online. A film about the "Cockleshell Heroes" as they were called was released in 1957 with Trevor Howard. Only 2 returned alive. When I reach Royan a queue of cars has built up for the ferry and I wait with the other cyclists, the most I have seen together, for the ferry to arrive. The wind has been strong all day and the ferry has trouble docking as the swell and the waves shunt it from side to side. It doesn't look that safe. I think the lorries on the bridge have knocked my mood for today as normally I wouldn't bother. We are soon on the boat but as it tries to manoeuvre it rolls to one side as the waves hit it. No-one else looks worried so I think this must be normal. The crossing is wild but after 35 minutes we land on the other side of the Gironde estuary.

After another few miles I see the Atlantic Ocean. I've arrived at Sulac-sur-Mer a bustling little seaside resort town with lots of cafés and restaurants. The town has its own Statue of Liberty made from the original mould. I arrive at my accommodation which is run by two guys – one of whom owns the property that has been in his family for three generations. He tells me how he used to visit his grandmother here and is obviously really proud to be living in the same house as her. The décor is amazing, modern with lots of sea themed ornaments and decoration. Finally, I manage to get bathroom scales and find my weight is now 6lbs different. Except I'm heavier. Could it be flab to muscle?

Figure 15 Sulac-sur-mer

I venture out in the evening and now it's pretty cold with the wind so I wear my rain jacket. Nothing is open and my choice of dining is limited. The only place that is busy is the Vietnamese restaurant in the casino so I choose that. It's been a long day cycling and I return to my hotel along the deserted seafront and look forward to tomorrows journey to a place I have been before.

Day 12, Tue, Soulac-sur-Mer 50 miles completed.

CHAPTER 15 I FACE SNOTTER MY POLISH FRIEND.

Today's cycle was supposed to be a gentle flat cycle by the beaches and sand dunes down the Atlantic west coast. Instead it was up and down the tarmac path over sand dunes and through miles of forest.

I met a new friend called Jerzy from Poland who was keen for company. It made the miles and miles of forest, into the wind, much more bearable. He was a speed freak and I had to up my pace. We passed by quite a few nudist beaches with their wicker screening but it was early, overcast and off season so little activity there. It's a bit boring today as we cycle through miles and miles of pine forest slightly inland so we don't see the sea. Every so often the track snakes to the coast through a resort and then back into the trees.

I don't know why my nose runs when its windy but it does. Streams and streams. I went for my hankies as it started again but as I turned to get the hanky the wind caught the snot and it ended up in Jerzy's face. An international incident. I said nothing and neither did he as he wiped it from his face. The Polish are great people and for some reason Jerzy insisted buying me a beer and some coffee.

He was a photographer who lived in Paris and told me many tales of his photography business. He is 62, faster than me on a bike and off to see his daughter in Bayonne. A common theme to many people I have met on this trip is their impression that an obsession for money has taken over. Jerzy felt that many more people were like this and the pursuit of more and more money had made people forget what is important in life. Even his neighbours who once chipped in to help everyone now just sit in their houses, surveying their property. We ate lunch by

Lake Lacanou and he is interrupted by a phone call that he conducts in Russian. So he speaks at least four languages. He cracks on and I sit on a bench on the beach by the lake booking my accommodation. But today it is gone – someone has booked it between breakfast and lunchtime. Now I have to try and find somewhere else. I then use the comparison site Trivago to find the cheapest places and decide to go to the hotel to ask for their cheapest room. A previous hotel owner suggested I do that as he doesn't have to pay the big companies.

The hotel I'm hoping to stay in is some kind of holiday resort and reception is closed till 4, so I have to wait to book in. I go down to the sea front and take a photo at stairs onto the beach at Lacanou a famous spot we all visited on cycle trip a few years back. Gordon swam in the sea here. He loves splashing about in water and was looking forward to getting to the Atlantic that day. I send him a postcard from the spot.

I cycle back to the hotel that I know has rooms and ask the reception desk for their cheapest room. It's 20% lower than the cheapest price online so I agree quickly. The receptionist even gives me a ground floor room so I can wheel my bike in.

I'm out of money now and the days are so exhausting, I do not want to camp, as it is extra luggage and more exertion. The 2 a.m. trudge to the toilet block is privation too far. My granny died twenty-one years ago and left me some money that I have never used, waiting for the special moment when using that money seemed right. So, I dip into the money now to fund my hotel stays. She would be happy about that and I really don't want to camp this late in the trip. Thanks gran!

Tonight, I watch Andy Murray on TV win his French Open match and he is now through to the semi-final on Friday. His interview in France is the same monotone English and not a word of French.

He's only been in France like 100 times. Also bought a bottle of Large Malartic as this area is full of wineries and it would be wrong to not try it. Sitting eating my bread and cheese for tea I watch the forecast for tomorrow and it's back up to 32 degrees. I decide to leave very early in the morning and make arrangements with reception.

Day 13, Wed, Lacanou 47 miles completed.

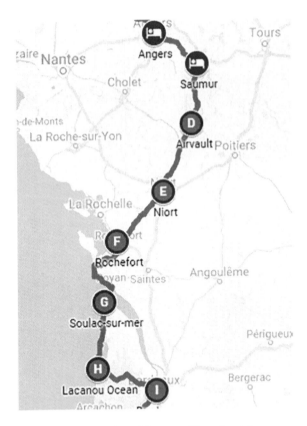

Figure 16 Map of the second leg of my trip

For the second leg of my trip I have cycled through

Angers
Saumur
Airvault
Niort
Rochefort
Sulac-Sur-Mer
Lacanou

CHAPTER 16. THE KINDNESS OF STRANGERS

Pretty boring day cycling a straight track on a converted railway line to Bordeaux. Nothing at all happened. Did you know the Burdie burn in Edinburgh is named after Bordeaux? Burdie=Bordeaux. It's at little France in Edinburgh. Many Scots merchants did business with the Bordeaux wineries and both the Irish and Scots ran a few vineyards. The track today is tarmac on an old railway line and is straight and uninteresting. The heat builds throughout the day and I decide to cool down in a McDonalds. I never go to McDonalds normally but they have air conditioning and I need the coke for energy.

There's 214km to go and barring accidents I'm hoping to make it. My thoughts have turned to how to get home with my bike. The train prices are now a lot dearer as I am close to the departure date. In January a train from Biarritz to Paris was €19 but now its €90 The bike bus which runs from Biarritz to the UK is an option but doesn't go as far north as Scotland. Ryanair flights are £30. I email some bike shops to see if they can box my bike to take on a plane. All but one gives a negative. However, Martin invites me to go along to his shop to discuss. Long story short he will box the bike for free and I arrange for DHL to pick it up. I book my flight home which is 2.5 hours and there will be no hassle with getting a boxed bike to the airport as DHL are taking it.

Tonight, I'm in Bordeaux in an AirBNB in the Bastide. Bastides are fortified areas built by Edward II to protect English interests in France and this area of France was English for 400 years. Mind you the kings of England spoke French for 400 years so I am not sure which way round we should be looking at this. The area is surrounded by wineries and the famous wine town of St Emillion. Two of the wineries were owned by Scots and others Irish so a real international heritage.

The house in the Bastide is the best of the trip and brand new, on 2 levels with a garden out back so I can do a washing. At home I do all my own washing and ironing and have never wanted my partner to do the washing. She works as well as me. I am now used to the French top loaders although I have to guess some of the program options. Washing machines are getting very complicated and it is difficult to guess what option needs selected. Even in the UK my new machine comes with an LCD push panel with far too many options. The panel will give out before the machine does and makes it so confusing. Mechanical dials are less likely to fail and how many options do you need? Anyway, the washing gets done and hung in the designer garden out back.

I go into town for the happy hour bars and meet a woman in a bar on the main street in Bordeaux. She is married and has flown into Bordeaux alone. The "after work" drinks keep coming – half price lagers - and we end up going for a curry. The worst curry ever it has to be said with waiters who are over attentive and whose patter is insincere. We sit at a small table in a narrow, crowded alley in the tourist quarter. Without warning, and not forecast, a huge electrical storm spikes across the sky with lightning and thunderous booms. The rain starts to come down in huge slow-motion droplets that threaten to become a monsoon at any moment. We both rush back to the safe dryness of the large house in the Bastide I have rented and we soon fall asleep in the large double bed.

Day 14, Thu, Bordeaux 43 miles completed.

Chapter 17. I walk into a TV studio

I wake up after my good night last night. The spectacular thunderstorm with forked lightning which was not forecast nor was the rain which soaked my washing that I had left outside. I was staying in the Bordeaux Bastide where the houses are cheap and are being bought up and renovated as an up and coming area. Bordeaux is an old town with narrow streets and they have transformed their city by banning cars from the centre and putting in trams. Fast and clean and every few minutes. Dedicated cycleways crisscross the town.

My wife is still asleep and I get up to go for breakfast as she loves croissants. There was a good start to the day as the woman in the local patisserie slipped an extra croissant in for free. "They are too small for you so I give you extra" she says in French with a big smile.

Figure 17 The extra free croissant

I was still looking for coffee and passed the TV7 studios. This is one of France's big TV channels but more akin to channel 5 in terms of reach than the BBC. French TV I find boring as it can be talk shows, cartoons and quizzes most of the day. I notice the open doors and wander in to have a look only to find myself in the studio behind the presenters where they are doing the review of the papers that morning. No warning, no security, nothing. I search the website later to get the film of me but they don't put the morning shows on line.

Bordeaux still has the old town gate entrances to the old city and has the longest pedestrian shopping street in Europe. Their signature tourist attraction is "the mirror", a football sized area filled with a thin film of water, which has special fountains that go off every so often. The water acts as a mirror and you can take photos of the large classical French palaces and museums which are reflected in the water. Small children run around enjoying the coolness.

Figure 18 Bordeaux mirror with mist

My wife enjoys shopping so we soon find ourselves on the long shopping street and I take a photo of a Wallace fountain that has found its way to Bordeaux. The Wallace fountains are famous in France and all over the world. They are of a distinct design, no taller than 8 feet with three Greek classical women holding up a conical roof and the water is dispensed from under this covered structure. Richard Wallace was the illegitimate son of an English baronet and had inherited some money. He lived in Paris in the late1860's and in 1872 two years after inheriting money from his late father he donated 50 drinking fountains to allow the poor people of Paris fresh water. During the siege of Paris, the year before he organised relief for the defenders. The aqueducts to Paris had been destroyed in the siege and water was now more expensive than beer. The fountains allowed the poor to drink and even today the homeless and destitute of Paris use the still working fountains to drink. So, he is a bit of a hero to the French and you can find streets named after him near the Bois de Boulogne in Paris. If you are in Paris Google the Wallace fountains location and taste the drinking water. They have also spread to other cities around Europe and the world and I encountered one in Geneva near the reformation wall last year.

Figure 19 Wallace Fountain

A few people gave me money to buy something when away so my aunt and uncle's money was used to buy lunch in "il Nocino", one of Bordeaux's best restaurants. As ever the lunchtime menu du jour gives excellent value for a man with a Scottish wallet and the service and quality was as expected in the famous Rue Saint-Remi, with its many upmarket restaurants.

In the evening it was happy hour drinks then out to one of the restaurants in the Chinese quarter and much better food than the horrible curry the night before.

A relaxing day and a rest I needed. Now planning the last few days of the trip to the finish line. My anxiety levels rise again as I am very close.

CHAPTER 18. THE HEAT IS ON AND I LOSE MY AMAZON TABLET

The temperatures have jumped up 10 degrees this morning so the big challenge is to get the cycling done by lunchtime. By 11am it was 26 and by 2pm 33 degrees. Breakfast is a Catalan pie which I discover is a rhubarb tart.

I left Bordeaux later than usual after seeing my wife on the bus to Bordeaux airport so it's a shorter cycle today given the heat. Quite a busy road but mostly cars which generally give you space. Still I get nervous when I hear the juggernauts behind and about to pass at speed.

I'm entering another national park – the Parc Natural Regional des Landes de Gascogne so its miles of trees and very flat. I make very good time on the tarmac with the wind behind me and reach my destination, Salles, for a late lunch. The small village of Salles has 4 places to eat and the one I pick is family run, on the outskirts, in a converted gatehouse to a chateau. I select a table outside and the daughter of the family who is about 14 takes my order in perfect English despite me speaking French to her. I reason, she has seen my Hibernian hat which says "Edinburgh" and it is not my poor French. The food is excellent and cheap as is the wine. The restaurants in the out of the way places have been consistently good and the prices reasonable.

Figure 20 Typical French lunch on cheap menu du jour

The choice of accommodation in this area is not large. I could never have managed a tent on top of everything else. I packed my sleeping bag that I bought at Decathlon off home with my wife so I had less to carry and have given up any notion of sleeping rough. This small village had a choice of three places to stay and I plumped for the hotel by the river run by a Dutch couple. The Domaine du Pont de l'eyre is an old coaching house that has a relaxed family appeal to it. The Dutch couple "living their dream" seem as hard working as others I encounter on the trip. Another afternoon snooze. I phone Gordon to update him on the last couple of days and we speak for an hour.

Sigh. This morning I finish my book by Bryony Gordon the Daily Telegraph journalist who writes very honestly about the horrors of living with Obsessive Compulsive Disorder (<u>Mad Girl</u>) and go to start my new book this afternoon only to realise I left the Amazon Fire tablet on the floor, under the bed in the Bordeaux

Bastide. The attrition rate on this trip of lost items means that when I get to the end, I will have nothing to carry. The constant packing and unpacking and potential to leave something in the wrong place is pretty high.

I email the Airbnb people and they can't find my Amazon kindle I left in Bordeaux, so it's not looking good.

There is a supermarket across the road – the only shop I have seen in this small village - so it's bread and cheese for tea and a glass of wine downstairs before bed. I need to get up early tomorrow as the heat is back on.

Day 16, Sat, reached Selles 30 miles completed.

CHAPTER 19. MY BAG GETS LIFTED WHILE I'M IN THE SEA

One of the best days yet. I'm up at 6 a.m. to beat the heat as 33 degrees is the forecast. The owner has given me keys to unlock the hotel as no-one else is up. After letting myself out I lock up again and hide the keys under a flower pot as agreed. It's cool at this time and I'm hoping to make good progress.

I was glad to leave the remote Salles and head west towards the Atlantic on the forest track. My routine now is cycle for 2 or 3 hours then stop to get breakfast. The national Park Landes de Gascogne is flat and the trees stop the wind. The route I planned is busy with traffic so I find tarmacked forest paths to go on but it's a longer ride. The wildlife has changed ever since I crossed that terrifying bridge with lizards now the normal roadside scuttle - and I didn't know cockroaches were so big! I head west to Sanguinet on the edge of the Bicarasse lake so I can then pick up the north/south Atlantic cycleway. It was not my intended route but I really do not enjoy juggernauts passing me so I take the longer road which is quieter. If I get tired I will stop along the way. As with other days I have nothing booked when I set off in the morning but I am more confident of my abilities now. I stop at Bicarasse after 23 miles for breakfast and find a nice little café in the middle of a market. Bicarasse is famous for making seaplanes and in the second world war was a base for German Dornier 24 aircraft that took off from the large "Hydrobase de Bicarasse". French military rockets are tested here and every so often I come to a large fenced off area in the woods with "interdit" signs. More recently oil was discovered so various petrol companies, mainly from Canada have operations here.

For quite a while now I have seen the pilgrimage signs for the route to Santiago de Compostella. The church in Airvault with the underground fountain, was a stop-over point for pilgrims from that part of France. The bones of St James are buried in Santiago de Compostella and pilgrims from all over Europe travel on the many different routes that converge in Galacia, Northern Spain. As I get closer to the Spanish border, the signs for pilgrim's increase. Mimizan was also built as a stopping place for pilgrims but now it is famous for the beach and has a holiday resort. I reach the town at lunchtime and wander round the very busy streets looking at the prices of the restaurants. One street has an excellent French café with a three-course meal for just 12 euros. After a 53-mile cycle this is just what I need and I get a half litre of red and litre of water to go with it. I've quite enjoyed today, as it was flat and there was a lot to see along the way. After lunch I made my way to the ocean promenade and the long strip beach was packed. The temperatures are around 33 and the cool sea looks inviting. As I looked onto the beach a girl spoke to me asking if I needed help.

I have previous here. On a cycle trip around Lisbon with friends a couple of years before, I had left our cheap accommodation in the early hours to get a bottle of water. The heat had been intense and the accommodation had no air-conditioning. I was standing on the Placa Major - the main square in Lisbon - obviously looking a bit lost and a girl asked me if I needed help. Young people are very helpful and keen to practice their English. She even offered to take me to the shop that sold the water and down one of the narrow streets that make up Lisbon's old barrio streets. Then she assaulted me. It was a bit of a shock and I couldn't believe it was happening. I wasn't quite sure what was happening but I got her hands out my trousers, pushed her away and ran off down the street. It was all a bit surreal but a lesson learned. On reflection some of the conversation should have warned me but I thought it was just normal chit chat.

So, in Mimizan a girl offers to help me as I'm looking for somewhere to get my swimming shorts on. She tells me she can take me to a toilet, where I can get changed. First of all, she spoke to me and secondly, she's offering to take me to a toilet. I feel bad at being wary and doubting the kindness of this stranger but I'm wiser now - at least in this one area. The toilet is one of the metal cubicles just off the promenade car park. I say thanks and go to padlock my bike removing my bag of valuables and she wanders off.

I reckon I can get into the toilet, changed and out in 3 minutes so not enough time to get my gear stolen off the bike. The toilet is one of the ones that is hosed down every time someone uses it. Everything is soaking wet and it's a struggle to get changed without getting my clothes wet. When I come out my gear is still there and I wheel the bike down to the promenade.

I was desperate to get into the water, so I padlocked my bike and took off one of my two pannier bags with my valuables to the beach. The beach is 14 miles long with huge Atlantic waves crashing in. There are two blue flags marking an area where you can go into the sea and they have three life guards. I walked down onto the beach suddenly realising that it was a topless one. I've never been on a topless beach before amongst so many people of all ages. I went to where the lifeguards were and ask if I could leave my bag by their beach buggy but they refuse.

I decided to just leave it on the beach in full sight of me from the water's edge. It was very sunny so I kept my top on so I did not get sunburn then run into the ocean. It was magic in the heat having the waves crash into you. I spent 90 minutes in the water. My bag was on the sand in full view with all my valuables.

As I looked round at one point I saw a man walking away with my bag with my passport, money, phone and everything of value. I waded to the shore to give chase but I could not move fast in the water up to my waist. Adrenalin kicks in. I'm watching him move inland, away from the water with my bag and then suddenly he drops it in the sand. He was moving it back from the water's edge! Phew.

Figure 21 Mimizan beach

I get to my accommodation at 4 p.m. and decide to lie down for two minutes. I wake at 7! Back into town for food only to find it deserted and all the restaurants closed. It's a day tripper resort. I find a cheap takeaway still open and get some noodle dish. When I get back to the hotel I ask the owner for a glass of wine. My French is better but he comes back with an opened bottle. I'll find out in the morning what that cost. A pint of wine here is cheaper than the equivalent in beer so here's hoping. Two days to get to the end point!

Day 17, Sun, Mimizan 55 miles completed.

CHAPTER 20. I STAY IN A SURFERS HOSTEL BY A NUDIST BEACH

Up at 5am UK time to beat the heat and complete the cycle before it gets too hot. Once again, I have to let myself out the hotel before it opens to get on the road. Got lucky as it is overcast this morning. This has been the longest physical endurance test in my life with a number of issues to deal with. I am not sure of the dividing line between bravery and stupidity. I'm not a brave person so we are probably veering on the stupid side of things. I get up from a desk with months of inactivity, get on a brand-new bike with my Scottish clothes and then take a train to the north of France with nothing booked and a general sense of heading south. I do this during the English school's bank holiday break and a heatwave. I like to think of it as ingenuity, determination and perseverance. However, two days out I hit my biggest problem yet. I was in quite a bit of pain yesterday. Stop reading now if you are squeamish. Does anybody ever do that? Skip the next paragraph and page. You have been warned!

So, the last 10 miles were agony yesterday. Absolute agony. No laughing when I tell you about my nipple chafing. I've never experienced this before but both my nipples have been rubbed red raw with a bit of blood coming from one. Absolute agony but then I'm a man. Every turn of the pedal and my moobs bounce up and down against my shirt material. That was yesterday and everything was much better when I switched to a cotton shirt. I wondered what to do for today and considered a bandage round my chest. When I woke up in the morning, things were a lot better so I will make do with a cotton shirt. Much better and only uncomfortable. Gives me the heebie jeebies to look at them. Urgh.

Saw a lot more pilgrims on the Camino de Santiago today. One pilgrim was actually asleep on the cycle path and I nearly ran over him. He was surprised to be woken at 6am. I then took a wrong turning in the forest and travelled up a hill for 10 minutes, to what turned out to be a dead end. On the way back, I was startled to see a man hanging from a tree. He had obviously wandered up this track to escape the attention of passers-by. He had tied a hammock between two trees and this was his tent/bed. Another pilgrim. Lots of signage along route for this 1000-year-old pilgrimage.

So, lots of trees, a few towns and quite a bit of cloud cover which is welcome. I stop at a campsite shop in the forest which sells croissants but no coffee. Some water washes it down and I am on my way. The Atlantic Ocean is to my right as I travel south but the pathway is inland, in forest and rarely do I see the sea. I make good progress and decide to choose my accommodation. I strike it lucky as I get a whole room in a surfer's hostel with en suite bathroom for 12 pounds. I think there must be some mistake.

When I arrive, there is no one in charge around and one of the other surfers shows me to a room that is "probably mine". I'm free to wander round the whole house with kitchen, dining area, living room with flat screen TV and Xbox.

Gradually the hostel fills up with 20 something surfers, bronzed and muscular. I fit in well.

I prefer the hostel atmosphere as you can chat to people. I meet a German, Australians and a Brazilian and within 10 minutes of arriving, I am offered a free lunch and free surf lessons. One guy started telling me how his grandfather lived in Hunterston and then moved to Brazil. I hope it was me mentioning Scotland that got that conversation started. Half the surfers are girls and I feel old enough to be their grandfather. They don't wear a lot of clothes round the house and I concentrate on looking at their eyes.

I'm told I have a trustworthy demeanour. As I said on an earlier trip this year I lost my bag of valuables (I bet you are surprised) and the insurance company paid out on the basis of a phone conversation - no forms or evidence required, because I sounded "trustworthy" the insurance agent said. I do like to be honest and sometimes it infuriates those around me. On a previous cycling trip we went to a bar on the Somme and ordered food and drinks. It was a set meal "menu du jour" type thing. When the bill came they hadn't charged for the drinks and I insisted we tell them. My friends were not happy as they would also have to pay more but as the trip leader I got my way and told the waitress that she had undercharged us. "mais non" she says in French, "we took the drinks off your bill as you didn't have a starter" If I hadn't asked we wouldn't have known they gave us the drinks for free! I'm not sure where this sense of honesty comes from – one of my friends said the term was "righteous", which they did not mean in a complimentary way. My favourite, was a hitch-hiking trip to the Munich beer festival where we camped at the big municipal site. I was 20 and again I was the trip organiser. And again, my friends railed against my policy of paying what's due. In Germany, all public transport works on an honesty system and my view was we should abide by that. My cash strapped student friends didn't see things my way and my compromise was that if we were wearing our kilts we were representing Scotland and should pay what's due. If we were wearing jeans then fine. When we got on the bus at the campsite it was full of Aussies, Argentinian's Italians, Kiwis and a smattering of other nationalities. One stop down the line, the bus was met by 6 ticket inspectors. We were the only people on the bus with a valid ticket and everyone else got an on the spot fine. I felt vindicated.

Anyhow, here and now, this Australian cyclist guy who announces himself as Ben, arrives at the surf hostel. He knows nothing of my kilted hitch-hiking history or my insurance company conversations. But he hands me his wallet, passport and phone to look after. Because I look trustworthy he says.

Figure 22 Ben hands over his wallet

Then he says he is sleeping with me, as there are no other beds. I knew the 12-pound deal was too good to be true. He also finds out the local shops are now closed, so I offer to cook him tea and share my bottle of wine. He goes off to the beach and I give him a time to return.

The surfers hostel is by the nudist beach, so I go up to have a look but access to the nudist beach is controlled to prevent voyeurs, so I go to the other one to watch the surfers. I wonder what the French is for voyeurs.

I get back to cook the tea. I chat to a girl surfer from Stuttgart and talk about my visit there in January. I thought it was a lovely town but people in the surfer's hostel appear to be in a hurry to leave their homes, as other places are better. I like travelling but am always glad to get home to Edinburgh.

Another aspect to my character is that if I say food will be ready at a particular time, I make sure it is. And I expect people to be at the table for it. Ben does not arrive. I open the wine and start eating the pasta when he floats in oblivious to the social crime committed. Aussie rules I think. He tells me about the publishing company he works for in Tokyo and how he is over for work. His iPhone is in Japanese so now I'm impressed. And, unlike other Aussie's I've met he doesn't drink a lot of my wine. The hostel owner arrives and says there is a room for Ben upstairs, so he moves his stuff out and I get the room to myself.

I sit down to write my blog and I calculate the total distance so far for the first time. I find that I have passed the 1000km mark! 1020km completed today. Woo hoo. Lots of generous people and the RNIB fund passes £1700. A very good day.

Day 18, Mon, Seignosse 49 miles completed.

Chapter 21. Deja vu

So, a big day and anxiety as it is the last day and I hope that nothing goes wrong. After 18 days of cycling, many lost items, saddle sores, lip sores, exhaustion, heat stroke and chaffed, bloody, nipples I have one day to get to the end. The surfer's hostel was a perfect last night and I enjoyed the company of the people there. Ben and I had breakfast with lots of jam but he didn't get ready to go in time so I left without him. Ben was late for everything and if I am honest I was keen to do my last days cycle to Biarritz solo

The other surfers were very kind and came out to the gates to see me off. They were really nice. Twenty minutes later, I was back as I'd left my mobile charger. Ben still wasn't ready so I'm off without him, again!

Today was like a microcosm of the entire trip, as I cycle through forest, by canal, through housing estates and then along roads beside juggernauts. How does life turn out like that? A summary of the entire trip in one day.

I stopped in Bayonne to have a look and was glad I had not stayed there. The trip into town was heavy with traffic and on a poorly maintained road, so it was not that enjoyable. A large church in the centre but not much life about it so I was soon off.

As I set off from Bayonne it was as if some film script writer had contrived a perfect ending as Giles, the Medicins San Frontiers doctor, from the cycle at Rochefort came cycling up behind me and we did the final 5 miles into Biarritz together. What a perfect finish chatting and swapping stories on that final stretch up and down along the coast. And then there it was the sign for Biarritz. We shook hands Giles having travelled from Roscoff and myself from Normandy. I had completed 1078 KM (666 miles) and we took our photos. I changed into my RNIB shirt for the photo – the fund now stood at £1745 which is much more than the £150 I originally thought about. Giles took the photos in my RNIB shirt. Then I changed into my Hibs football shirt – I wanted the final leg to be in my Hibs shirt. Persevere is the motto of Leith and the football club I support and that's what I had done. Giles asked "any more shirts?" I had worn three in the space of 3 minutes.

Figure 23 Two shirts

We said au revoir and I started the final run into the town centre in my Hibs shirt and hat which was magnificent. I was so happy and elated I had made it. I went to the main beach and sat at the most salubrious restaurant on the sea front – "the café de la Plage" with its ornate chandeliers inside and multitude of tables outside. I ordered a beer for £6. I phoned Gordon first (sorry mum). I had done it. I described the scene and the feeling. We were both a bit emotional.

We said goodbye and I went down to the Biarritz main beach to have a celebration beer in one of the promenade cafes.

I had sat down at the only table free which happened to be in front of the sole shower facility on the topless beach and I watched an endless procession of "Tales of the Unexpected" auditions.

Figure 24 Tales of the unexpected

I phoned my mum and she was a bit emotional. She had turned from someone who didn't want me to go as it wasn't fair on my wife, to my number one fan, taking her Samsung tablet round town with her and showing anyone who sat next to her on the bus what I was doing. Every lunch time with a crony, they got a monologue of my latest adventure and what had happened. My wife, I phoned after she finished work and now I was looking forward to getting home.

After my drink on the beach I went to the apartment I had rented. The woman arrived promptly and I was taken to an attic flat in an old French building from the last century. The lobby of the apartment block was large and full of marble, like the lobby of a hotel and the lifts like something from the 1930's. "The lift does not go all the way to your floor" she said and when we got to the lift it was another flight of stairs to, where I presume, the servants slept in the last century. The roof came down at an angle in my studio flat but it was all I needed and was modern and clean. Windows looked out over the roof tops of Biarritz and a flock of pigeons perched. For some reason the toilet had an electrical cable plugged into the wall and no flush mechanism. I tried for ages to get this to work but eventually gave up. Why would a toilet be plugged in? I did need to flush and eventually I found a button on the bit that attaches the toilet seat. The toilet then made a noise like a meat grinder. I kept the seat down.

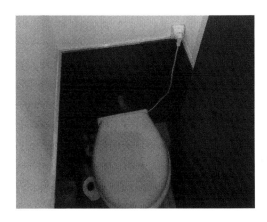

Figure 25 Toilet that needs plugged in

Lunch was a pizza place with a bottle of wine for the same price as a glass on the seafront – they only sold by the bottle so I had to take it. Then it was back to the flat for a snooze. I am so happy.

In the evening, I found this really great Breton bar with 30 different Breton beers and a great atmosphere. I had my fish and chips for 10 euros and sampled the various beers on offer during the happy hour. It was a great evening, with lots of Breton half price beer and the adventure was over. Or so I thought. More was to come.

The final few days had been completed through

Lacanou Ocean,
Bordeaux,
Salles,
Mimizan,
Seignosse,and then to
Biarritz.

Figure 26 Map of the last leg of the trip

Still carrying on blog until I'm home...

Day 19 Tue Biarritz 32 miles completed. I have cycled 1078km 666 miles and raised £1745.

Chapter 22. A pianist, an ironing board and Hibs supporters branch

My head is sore for the first time on the trip after a late night in a wonderful bar that sold many different IPA beers. Lots of money coming into the JustGiving page again which is amazing. I'm in an attic studio right, in the centre of Biarritz and the roof is also home to pigeons. I make sure the windows get closed before going out, as a pigeon can make a lot of mess.

I decided to use more of my gift money to treat myself and go to the swanky Cafe de La Grande Place on Biarritz beach. I have breakfast and watch the early morning surfers. Strangely, the breakfast was cheaper than anywhere else in town. I paid and the waitress bit the bill so her teeth marks show it was paid.

There is a continuous roar of waves crashing on the beach and, the surfers are all experienced with their stylish wetsuits and boards. Then I spot this ginger haired Scottish type guy heading for the water with a pair of baggy shorts and what looks like an ironing board. The Alf Tupper of the Biarritz surfers.

Surfing involves a lot of patience, waiting for the right wave and then getting into it, kneeling on your board and then trying to stand. Alf tries and tries but he just can't get his ironing board to float. Everyone else is doing Hawaii 5-O.

I wait and wait until 45 minutes pass. He still has not surfed. I need to go. Then this huge wave comes, he gets on his ironing board and he does it. Absolutely fantastic.

Figure 27 Alf Tupper on a surf board

I check out the apartment and head off to meet the Biarritz Branch of the Hibs Supporter Club for lunch. Barry lived in Edinburgh growing up and still gets to the occasional game, flying home from the south of France. His wife Nadine is French and they take me to the market quarter of Biarritz that I never knew was there. Round the market there are lots of little restaurants selling wonderful food, including Basque cuisine. I see many Basque flags in this area. Barry wants to know how I managed to get shares in Hibs. Mohammad Ali gave me the money to buy shares I tell him! My friend runs a "Deadpool" which is a celebratory list of people picked at random and if one of them dies then you collect money. Fifty-two people put in five pounds a month with names drawn at random out of a hat. I had Mohammed Ali and when he passed away I got the Deadpool money. I didn't need the money so I bought shares in this fantastic football club, Hibernian FC. Mohammad Ali bought them for me which I think is nice. The shares will pass down through my family along with the Mohammad Ali story, so that's good too.

I also tell Barry about the deal Macron has made with Hibs. I thought this Macron was the French president but is actually an Italian sportswear company. In France President Macron has started a new political party called "en Marche" made up of novice politicians but "real" people and they had a landslide victory on Sunday. I wonder if he is part Scottish with the MacRon name? Probably in the same way that O'Bama is Irish. Another constant question from Europeans on this trip is why did Britain vote for Brexit? They cannot understand and every conversation turns to this including todays.

It was a wonderful lunch with some great company and a nice end to the trip. Barry and Nadine insisted on paying for the meal despite my protestations.

I leave in plenty time for the train. I'm looking forward to travelling on the high-speed TGV but you need to book your bike on and it can only be done at the station which is two miles out of town. When I get there, there are no places left for a bike so I need to wait two hours for the next train. Luckily the French put pianos in railway stations for the public to play so I'm entertained by a succession of players. It's amazing how many people here are good at the piano.

The train arrives exactly two hours later and so it's off to Bordeaux. Did I mention my Amazon tablet was found under the bed in Bordeaux? Pierre arranges to meet me at Bordeaux la Gare and hands it over. I have books and films for tomorrow. Yes! I cycle to the AirBNB accommodation I have booked, which is next to the University and within sight of the main square in Bordeaux, with a fake Scottish pub. The area is not particularly nice and my suspicions are raised when I see the number of locks on my door. When I get into the apartment, I discover my accommodation is a student flat in an old apartment block, with no light in the bathroom. The toilet is the same as the one in

"The Young Ones". The apartment is right next to Victoire and University of Bordeaux so cheap drink but the worst place I've stayed on the trip. The security on the doors unnerves me and the area is a bit run down. 32 degrees at 8:30 p.m. and very humid. Looking forward to tomorrow and penultimate blog update and head out for a couple of drinks.

I manage to get to the "Scottish" pub during after work happy hour. After a couple of beers, I go for a wander and some lassie who speaks to me, gets me into the comedy club for free. People always seem to speak to me and it turns out she is a barmaid in a club in the university quarter. The club is set up like an Edinburgh Fringe show – its crowded with not enough seats and very hot. It seemed popular and everyone was laughing at jokes about the Italians. I didn't understand enough so didn't stay long. The Italians do not seem popular. I couldn't find anywhere I wanted to eat so settled on a McDonalds. I usually avoid them but it's my encore.

So, after only 2 beers and a hamburger I head back to the apartment to find the main door closed and my keys do not work. Phone battery at 10%. I'm desperate for the toilet. There is a contact fob but it keeps flashing red and won't open the door. I check the address -102 – and that's correct. Two workmen try to help. Weird that workmen are out at midnight. They have their bright dayglow yellow jackets on and they try to help me get into the stair.

I can't believe it. On my last night. The keys don't work! I'm locked out.

With my last battery juice, I update my blog to say "Any relatives/ friends reading this know that things always turn out well for me, so no worries. "

Figure 28 Workman tries to get me in after getting locked out

The owner of the flat when I phone them tells me to push the door harder but it doesn't work It turns out I am at the wrong door. There are two doors with 102 above them. Its 102b I should be at 10 feet down the road. What a night! I slump into bed. At 1:30 a.m. I get a text from my mum asking if I am alright. She has been reading the blog and the fact that I am locked out has worried her. I'm impressed and surprised she is reading my blog at this time of night. I go back to sleep and wake up early due to the heat.

Morning. I now have to pack 3 weeks luggage into one bag and get on the Ryanair flight, looking like a Michelin man, to avoid paying for hold luggage.

I leave my keys, hidden in a box on the landing and bid farewell to my "Young Ones" student flat.

I cycle off to see Martin at the Culture Velo Merignac bike shop, who will post my bike home. But when I get there I am told they do not have time to pack my bike and I will have to do it. This is a disappointment, as I understood they were doing it for free and I don't actually know how to take my new bike apart. My last bike I had for 17 years and knew how everything worked but this one I needed help with. It has hydraulic brakes with fluid, so taking the wheel off is an issue. After offering them money they relent. Phew. They do not take the money though.

Figure 29 Magnificent Martin

It's a bit boring for the rest of the afternoon, as I kill time waiting for my flight. Lunch is in "Flunch", a buffet style chain restaurant in France that gives you a taste of various foods and allows you to heap your plate with whatever food they have. I linger there for a couple of hours, catching up with stuff on my phone before getting the number 1 bus to the airport. Everything is straightforward and I am soon climbing the steps onto my budget flight home for £29.

The flight is uneventful and I arrive at Edinburgh airport in good time, the budget airline trumpets, proclaiming another budget flight on time, as it lands. My wife and friends have arranged to meet me and I will be going straight off the plane into a taxi, to our local pub. I can feel my heart pumping faster as I head for the taxi. I'm looking forward to seeing everyone. The taxi pulls into the local pub car park and my heart is now bulging out my chest like the cartoon characters. Or at least it feels like that. I'm starting to feel emotional too. I slip in through the side door and scan the pub which has three separate large seating areas. I see everyone at the back of the pub and applause breaks out with a couple of cheers. Banners balloons, my family, my mum and friends. And Gordon. What a great homecoming. My favourite pint is delivered and once again a loud cheer breaks out.

It's fabulous to see everyone. Gordon's partner has written a poem and stands up to deliver it. Here it is;

THE CANNY TRAVELLER

Welcome home Andy, friends and family gather near. Raise your glasses to the canny traveller whom we love so dear.

You have been on an epic journey from the north to the south of France. Warm showers and shortbread in Luc Sur Mer commandoes in Caen to Flers.

Bed, commode and toilet roll, all within a bar. Snakes and dogs, and a lorry crash with cars.

Unusual meals in brown dish clothes, at riverside cafes. Chance meetings with local wildlife didn't get in your way.

You journeyed on booking rooms along the way. From nursery floors to chateaux's with 50 % extra to pay. You enjoyed the occasional glass of wine. Befitting a man who is in his prime.

You braved bad traffic and some bridges. Steep hills and heat , but no MIDGES!

French cuisine and local beer. But the nudist beach got the biggest cheer.

You had a challenge in keeping going, a solo trip much harder than you knowing.

But you have raised an enormous sum. We know it was worth the sores on your bum!

You've made some friends along the way. Martin the bike man who wouldn't let you pay.

And that nice polish man Jersy who you covered in snotter. He still bought you lunch couldn't have thought you a rotter.

We're all a bit surprised you actually made it home. Losing all your valuables may limit your right to roam.

You have had a few adventures and kept us up to date. Your blog has entertained us but especially Gordon your mate.

He really wanted to be with you but fate played a bitter hand. You certainly made him fell part of it and we're so pleased it turned out grand.

The money raised for the RNIB will surely help to pay. For
continued support from this charity who help the blind each day.

We hope you enjoyed your adventure and had some fun
along the way

Maybe one day we will join you doing it the
"ANDYWALLACE WAY"

After a few hours, we head for home and I slumped into my own
bed, with the woman from Bordeaux.

Chapter 24. I lose my bike

I go back to my work on the Monday and when I walk in in the morning my desk is covered in balloons, cards, a rubber ring and various pictures associated with France. A big Eiffel Tower is fixed to the top of my screen. I'm a bit overwhelmed at the kindness. My laminated certificate, proclaiming me better than Bradley Wiggins and Chris Froome is tied in a red ribbon.

Figure 30 My desk

I never realised how many people had followed the blog and around 450 people a day were reading my latest adventures with thousands of hits. Throughout the day and week people speak to me about events in the blog. I feel they are making more of it than they should. I went on a holiday without my friend and then decided to do it for charity. There was no grand plan. If I hadn't been sponsored I would not have completed the trip and I would have stopped after the first couple of days. If I hadn't been sponsored I would have got a train west from Airvault justifying that it's not cheating as I wasn't gaining anything as it was a tour de France type transfer. But one sponsor had said "no trains" and that was that. "North to South, top to bottom, up to down - they all feel downhill to me. Feet up and let it roll. No trains now. Stay safe!" It was like an incantation out of Harry Potter but the spell said "no trains now" Looking back this is the comment that made me complete the trip!

My favourite story was from a colleague who was on holiday herself in rural France and told me how she had driven into the nearest town to find Wi-Fi so she could read the next blog episode. Wow. In general, that was the reaction from people, how they enjoyed the blog and my honesty. "A cross between Mr Bean and Basil Fawlty" – and that was my mum that said that!

A number of bike donations came in after my return home and the fund went up to £3300, so much more than the £150 I originally thought. It is a good feeling.

The days passed and there was no news of my bike. The bike was going by DHL and you could track its whereabouts. All it said was, it has left Bordeaux and the expected delivery was on Thursday. Thursday came and went and no bike. I checked on line and the web site still said Paris as its location, with expected delivery Thursday. In common with many companies these days there is no one to speak to and it's an online form to declare a package missing. I had to describe the package in detail and wondered how they could lose such an item. DHL had lost it somewhere! I had to fill out a form, describing the contents and submit it. Two days later the bike was found in Belgium. What was it doing there? The next day it arrived home safe and well. Phew.

I never lost a single thing on the trip. Many things disappeared for a while but everything was returned eventually, sometimes after a 300-mile round trip to collect it, like the computer tablet. Gordon finished his radiotherapy and I've joined the gym near his house so we can both get fit. He still can't see and the future is unknown. I came back 4 pounds lighter from France but I think some flab has turned to muscle, as my clothes fit me better.

Over the next few months I put back on the weight I lost and more. After spending the summer in Scotland, I went to Eindhoven in the Netherlands for a weekend with the woman from Bordeaux. It was a £20 flight and I enjoyed the ambiance, renting a bike to cycle the countryside. As I wandered to the bike shop, I took a photo of the thousands of bikes at the train station. There are more bikes than people in The Netherlands. And I am careful to say the Netherlands and not Holland as north and south Holland are just 2 of 12 provinces and it's like calling Scotland, Wales and Ireland "England". Anyway, I'm taking a couple of photos of bikes and this woman of about 45 comes up to me and says she is a photographer and she would like me to be her model. I'm remembering the other approaches and she can see my suspicion so she points over to a people-carrier and a gazebo that is set up in the street. She is part of a project to put 6-foot-high photos of people in the pedestrian underpass at the station. So, I pose for her and she takes a variety of shots. I give her my email as she says she will send me the photo but I misspell the email and I don't know if my photo made the final cut. She seemed pleased when she took my photo, as she called over her colleague to look at my photo which she said was very unusual. The colleague says I have an interesting physique. So I carry on to get my bike and plan a route to the castle of Helmond in a town 20 miles away. Its a great cycle, following various canals and watching the many sporting rowers. It's canal side is wooded and interesting with little hamlets and photobook cottages every few miles. I pass some farm buildings and see lots of people coming out with bags laden with fruit. I wander in and see huge wooden pallets, full of hundreds of apples for sale at cheap prices. They sell a variety of apple called Elstar which I have never heard of, so I queue with my one apple and when I get to the till, the girl says I can have it for free. These kinds of apples I like.

At night we wander to the ethnic area of Eindhoven – it's always where you find the cheapest drink and food. In my experience, it's also where you encounter the greatest kindness. In my teenage days of working weekends in an Edinburgh family corner grocer, the best tippers were the poorest customers. On TripAdvisor I search for cheap eats then hit "map" to find where I should go. The area with the cheap eats is the area with cheap drinks. We found a corner bar, full of locals, who had been there since midday and it was now evening. The Dutch people are like Glaswegians and when you enter a bar, they chat to you. We had a great evening in the company of these locals followed by a delicious meal in one of the many ethnic restaurants in the street. Even in other countries my French luck follows me.

The week after, three of us, from the original four pub cyclists, go to Tuscany. As usual I am in charge of the accommodation bookings and as usual the adventures continue. Too many to write here (think France) but I am pleased to book two nights in Bologna city centre, at a really cheap price. The accommodation is in an old monastery retreat for monks named "Istituto dei Ciechi Francesco Cavazza". Quite often in Europe, former monasteries are converted to tourist accommodation, with long sounding names and quite often the monk's rooms are ideal. Except on this occasion what I thought was the name of an Italian

" Ciechi" is actually the Italian word for "blind" and "Istituto dei Ciechi" means "Institute for the blind". I have booked us into the Blind Institute for Bologna. I can't believe it.

When we arrive, they let us in and I think they are trying to make extra money letting sighted people stay. At breakfast my friend makes the mistake of pulling out a breakfast chair in line with the door and a succession of blind people bump into his chair. Some of the blind are learning to cope with their condition and one girl, when she turns around always seems to go off at 135 degrees instead of 180 to go back the way she came. She smacks into the wall. I see her a couple of times and once, when she is crossing a minor street, instead of getting to the other side, she loses her sense of direction and heads off down this side street. I feel guilty when I see her as my emotion is both humour at the slapstick nature of what I am watching and sadness for this poor girl struggling to operate in a world of darkness.

My friends suggest I continue the blog, as things like this keep happening. The second night, I manage to pick a beer in a bar that makes me very drunk, very quickly, only to find out later it is made from cannabis. That was a big mistake. The next morning, we take the train back to Lucca but find the trains are on strike. Italians don't do all day strikes – it is by train region and only till 5pm. The train starts in Bologna but then stops in Prato, where we have to get off. Outside the train station I can find buses going east to Florence but not west to Pisa and Lucca, where we want to get to. I suggest cycling 15 miles to Florence and getting an intercity train or bus. It's the regional railways that are on strike. However, our passports are with the bike shop and we fly out tomorrow. A vote is taken and we decide to start cycling west, which is 40 miles plus to home and over two mountain ranges. I have to come up with a plan that takes us home – I have not researched the routes and need to find quieter flattish routes. The Apennine mountains, called "the backbone of Italy", snake their fingers across this area. This makes it difficult, as the only route is a dual carriage way, cut through the hills and it will be busy with lorries, buses and the like. We set off, leaving Prato down a quieter straight road, Roman in origin. It turns out to be Chinatown and the biggest I have seen in Italy. Mile after mile of Chinese shops and signs and people on the Via Pistoiese. We cycle for an hour and a half then find a bus station to see if they will take our bikes. It's 25 miles home and we have our luggage on the back of the bike. "Yes, the buses will take your bikes", the ticket office tells my friend so he buys three tickets. Forty-five minutes, later we are still in the bus mob (it's not a queue), shoulder to shoulder with 100's of people desperate to get on a bus because of the train strike. Security guards are at each door to the bus – Italian buses have multiple doors to get on and ticket validation at each door. We give up and decide to climb the mountain along a dual carriageway. I look at the minor roads but they snake up and down the steep mountain in an "s" shape and 40 plus miles is more than my friends have done for many years. The dual carriageway it is. Halfway up the hill, I see a truck with an open top rear and I chat to the driver. "My friend is a grandfather" I say in my poor Italian in an effort to get him a lift. My friend is struggling and walking his bike up the hill, his back hurting him. The driver laughs with me and I think I have a chance of getting my friend a lift, until the driver's boss turns up and everything goes formal. We carry on, up and up. At the top it's a snaking, single car width route into the next valley and I cycle out in the middle of the road so lorries and buses can't pass me. I don't care because after the bridge in France, I am more nervous of large vehicles passing me and when we come to a bend my speed means I already veer into the middle of the road. Near the bottom I have planned a country road but when we get there it is closed for repair. The main road is very busy and narrow, so I speak to the workmen and they agree to let us through. After 100 yards we have the road to ourselves, as no traffic can get past the works that have closed the entrance to the street.

We cycle through villages and hamlets and it's nice, enjoyable cycling. We reach our halfway point at Montecatine Terme and we are exhausted. I go to the train station to see if the situation has changed but still there are no trains. I spot a people carrier taxi. "Quanta costa para Lucca" I ask. "Sixty Euros" comes the reply in English. My friends force the money into my hand and we travel in comfort the last 25 miles home to the villa. My friend who stays in Lucca, says he will need a year to recover from my annual visit. So, my adventures continue.

CHAPTER 26. EPILOGUE - FRIENDS

The work on this book takes up my spare time, but I meet Gordon with other friends for breakfast every Wednesday before work. I explain that I am working on this book of my trip and I ask his permission to publish, which he grants. I call it my "vanity project". Thursday night is friend's night and an evening of food, chat and cards at our local pub which Gordon attends when he can. Two weeks ago, the manager comes up to our table after we have finished eating and asks us to go outside. The look on his face tells us something is wrong. I suspect my bike, padlocked outside, has been damaged. When we get outside all our bikes are gone and the locks left on the ground, cut through. My bike is stolen. I was gutted as was my pal. The CCTV pictures are clear with three 15-year-old boys, arriving and stealing the bikes. As a juvenile there is little chance of their being brought to court and the police have many other things to deal with. I am left without my bike. My campaign to get it back gains traction in social media and makes the local newspaper with its "Warning over bike theft 'crimewave' in Corstorphine" headline. But I soon realise I'm one person and about two high end bikes are stolen every day in Edinburgh with recovery rates next to zero. At the time of writing, it is still lost and I do not think I will be getting it back.

A week ago, I receive an email from Eindhoven. I won the modelling competition described in the previous chapter and there will be an opening ceremony to install my photo 8-foot-high outside the main railway station. The woman from Bordeaux says I look like a monkey, but it's a boost to my mood knowing that my picture is cheering up the people of Eindhoven. My life continues to take strange turns.

Friends are important in life, because they stick by you and I have always been lucky with my friends. The emotional and practical support they give you at times of hardship or just the laughs you share help you through life with perspective and humour. I take my lead from my friends and try to be as good a person as them. I've not always succeeded but I try. If you make mistakes you cannot change what is done but look forward and make the best of what you do in the future. At a human level most people are basically good and on my trip people were running after me to return my credit card, meeting me at railway stations to return my tablet. Many people were donating large sums of money and Ben handed over his wallet and phone to me 3 minutes after meeting me for the first time. The support given to me on the trip was incredible and I appreciated every comment and pound that was given. Texts and messages came in every day of the trip and the emotional boost that gave is difficult to describe.

Figure 31Monkey outside Eindhoven Railway Station

.

On my birthday in July, I decided I would make more of an effort to keep connections and invited friends and family to Edinburgh's oldest golf clubhouse for a drink and some free food, with an opportunity to play on the world's oldest continuously used pitch and putt course. I think this year has emphasized to me the importance of friends and families and to appreciate what matters in life. Gordon and all his family came along, as did many friends and family who supported me on the trip. Some people say I did a great thing but all I did was go on a holiday without my friend. However, the sponsorship and blog website created something that was unique and for me will never be repeated. I know from Gordon's family, the difference it made to him and for that I am glad. On my birthday, I was able to show some small appreciation for my friends and family. What better way to enjoy life?

Appendix A - The Supporters

This is the list of donors and their messages on the Just Giving site at https://www.justgiving.com/fundraising/andy-wallace7 What I never realised is, that the anonymous donors are only anonymous online and the fund raiser can see who they are and what they contributed. Some people who I know well, gave me money but did not want me to know about it and never told me to my face. Those that kept the amount secret I know what you gave and you were always generous.

Without the people below, I would never have achieved the cycle. To the person that said "no trains" you pushed me to the limit!

Lorraine & Gennaro	Good luck Andy. Looking forward o following your adventures!
Anonymous	
George	Good luck and have fun!
Marjory	Good luck!
Pam	Good for you. Xx
Marissa	Good Luck Andy! Thank u so much for everything u have done!! x
Monika	Good luck Andy!
Julie	Good luck and enjoy Andy :)

Martin Leadbetter	well done Andy - why do you have a bike made by a cigarette company ? Good for you and I hope you enjoy - and survive - the trip. It's a great thing you are doing.
Neil H	Well done and good luck Andy.. you 'wheely' are some 'machine' !
Juliet	Great cause, good luck and enjoy :-)
Neil Orr	Great cause for a really good friend, good luck.
Tracy	Wheely it Wallace! Good luck
Lamine Lachhab	Brilliant cause very inspirational Andy. Please tell Gordon I'm thinking about and asking for him.
Louise	Good luck Andy. Great cause in honour of a great person. :) xxx
Lorna	Brilliant thing to do in honour of a friend. Great cause. Good luck! x
Mary	Be safe, Andy. Hope you raise a fortune! We are with you all the way.
Shirley	Go Andy. Brilliant effort for a worthwhile cause. xx
Caroline	Good Luck!!

Kyle	Good luck Andy. Hope you take plenty of water for the days and find plenty of wine for the nights.
Barbara	Bonne Chance!
Kate	I hope the sun shines on you Andy!
Anonymous	fae Raymonds brother
Hari, Peter, and His Mugship	We're with you, Andy, on your quest. Stay safe .... and well-hydrated. :)
Kerry	Good luck Andy :-)
Kirsty B	A great cause, Andy. Good luck!
Mary Henderson	Money raised by NRS colleagues through the sale of books at the front reception of Ladywell House. Such a good thing to be doing Andy. Please pass our regards to Gordon.
Anonymous	
Jerry Nimmo	North to South, top to bottom, up to down - they all feel down hill to me. Feet up and let it roll. No trains now. Stay safe!
Elizabeth	Bon Voyage!
Fliss Rollings	Best of luck Andy! :-)
Moira S	Good luck Andy!

Jon Miller	Good luck with the cycle Andy!! Best - Jon Miller
Mike and Helen Hilton	
D Green	It's great that Gordon's got good friends like you helping him out. Smashing thing to do - hope the trip goes well.
Adrienne Pettie	All the best for your trip in aid of a wonderful organisation
Jan x	Well done Andy and Good Luck!
Sarah	Wishing you all the very best for a safe and enjoyable trip. Thank you for all your support. Best wishes.x
Anne Courtney	Good luck with the cycle in support of this great charity!
Sudeep Kumar	All the best Andy
David & Emma and Rachel & Dave	Good luck! Don't forget the sun cream and an emergency can of coke!
Anonymous	Very best wishes to Andy on this venture.

Anonymous	Great cause Andy - take my hat off to you for your efforts
	Heart felt wishes to Gordon, wishing him a successful recovery
	Craig Stewart
Anon	Allez Andy
Immy	Well done Andy, a very worthy cause.
Pauline Brown	Well done Andy!!! Will be some adventure.
David R	
Diane Paton	Good luck Andy
Lynne Mundell	Good Luck Andy...........will treat you to a pint of milk when you get back!
	.................keeeeeeeeep cycling!
Ewan and Lynn Gibson	Good Luck Andy!
Chez and Andy xxx	Very much respect xxxxxx
Glynis	Good luck Andy. Enjoy xx
Graeme Mc	Well done Andy.
Laura Steele	Good luck Andy. Enjoy your adventure x

Maureen & Len Morris	Well done Andy. Dreadful news about Gordon.
Shirley Black	Well done Andy!!!
Russell Fleming	Bravo Andy. Looks like an epic adventure for a good cause.
Fee	Good luck Andy, really enjoying the blog
Christine Baker	Just keep cycling !!
Jenny Hunt	Very impressive! Jenny, WRH
Gill and John Manchip	Keep going Andy you are doing a great job..
Vicky	Keep up the good work!
Raymondo	Well done to Andy. Gordy- we will all do this next year.
Damian	Good luck Andy :)
Frank	best wishes
Eileen, Jim, David, Mairi-Ann and Jamie	Amazing Andy. Keep going.
Anonymous	What an adventure, well done Andy!
Mark Rotton	Try not to lose too much (other than weight of course)

Irishkisser3	Well done in persevering, not like that first cycle round Scotland, sun, rain, snow, sand .....but hot conditions just as much a test!! Hopefully this will break target!Love Jessica, Alexandra & David
Neil Bowie	So sorry to hear about Gordon's problems, but I am sure what you are doing is making a huge difference to him and to others!
Myra & Alistair	Great effort Andy, just wish Gordon could be doing it with you. Good luck for the rest of the adventure.
Jim Clark	Good luck Andy. Hope it all goes smoothly and hoping very much that things get better for Gordon - one of the nicest guys I've had the pleasure to know.
Joan Brown	Well done Andy.
Linda Boyle	Well done Andy x
Lynda Ross	Andy what a fantastic thing you are doing. I just caught up with this
Steve Fordyce	Good job Andy.

Andy & Irene Atkinson	Well done Andy! Great cause and entertaining blog at thecannytraveller.wordpress.com.
Anonymous	
Anonymous	Keep going, Andy - and keep up with the great craic on the blog.
Karen Finnie	You're an inspiration Andy just so wish Gordon was on this trip with you but if all this love and support is anything 2 go by he will get back 2 the cyclin trips I'm sure luv xKx
Jamie Nixon	
T Couper	A very worth cause, happy cycling!
Janette Gibson	Thank you so much Andy for donating your time, effort and enlightening blog to such a worthy cause and encouraging Gordon to remain positive and strong throughout this hard time. See you soon .x
Colin Hunter	Extremely well done on the trip. Mammoth task and great achievement
Miranda	Well done Andy
Keith Dargie	Well done Andy. Fantastic effort and achievement!

Anonymous

Sandra & Ian Dunn	Congratulations Andy what an achievement somewhere like Kinghorn will be a walk in the park now!
Matty Duncan	Well done Andy! A great effort! Only the tip of the iceberg in terms of the support you've given Gordon. Top man!
Graeme Sutherland	Great achievement and great cause.

Anonymous

Rosemary (Gordon's neighbour)	What a wonderful thing to do Andy. Very well done to you.
Fiona	Well done Andy - from Fiona, Alex, Jamie & Olivia
Marie Kay	Andy, you are a hero.
Sarah	So overwhelmed by how much you have raised Andy. Thank you from the bottom of my heart.
Brian.	Wished I had come with you !!

Keith Adam

Jill	well done Andy xxx
Mum	Very pleased and proud at your achievement

Margaret and Arthur Manchester	well done
Grayham	Well Done, Andy. Great achievement
Pauline	well done
Anonymous football fan	congratulations
Raymond Wilson	Well done Andy
Val	Well done Andy. An amazing journey for such a worthy cause and you kept us all entertained with your blog. x
Jerzy Palgan	Great blog Andy and well done!
Peter Johnstone	
Scott Keir	Hope to see you soon Gordon
Garry Wallace	Well done on your efforts Andy and a great blog too!
Eddie Turnbull	Well done Andy amazing!
Ian Anderson	Good stuff Andy. Best wishes to Gordon.
Mary Henderson	That's you over £3000 including gift aid!
Robert Brown	Fabulous. Well done
Gary Berzins	Well done Andy. Sounded tough, but a great adventure!

Anonymous	Well done.
David Brownlee	Hi Andy, just heard about this from Keith. Thoughts are with Gordon. Great fundraising effort by you. Hope to be in touch soon.
Gerry Coppola	
Paula Coppola	Hi Andy. What an amazing thing you are doing and for such a worthy cause. Tremendous
John Simmons	A great feat, well done.
John	
Francis Thomas	Well done, Andy.
Janet Wallace	Well done!

About The Author

 Just a guy who wanted to publish a book. Live life, enjoy life. Thanks to Brian, Rachel and Karen for all your hard work and my wife for putting up with me.

Find out more at amazon.com/author/andrewwallace

Or visit https://thecannytraveller.wordpress.com/

Printed in Poland
by Amazon Fulfillment
Poland Sp. z o.o., Wrocław